T0271585

Urban Garden Design

Transform your outdoor space into
a beautiful and practical escape

Kate Gould

Photography by Helen Fickling

Kyle Books

An Hachette UK Company
www.hachette.co.uk

First published in Great Britain in 2019 by
Kyle Books, an imprint of
Octopus Publishing Group Limited
Carmelite House
50 Victoria Embankment
London EC4Y 0DZ
www.kylebooks.co.uk

ISBN: 978 0 85783 4874

Distributed in the US by Hachette Book Group,
1290 Avenue of the Americas, 4th and 5th Floors,
New York, NY 10104

Distributed in Canada by Canadian Manda
Group, 664 Annette St., Toronto, Ontario, Canada
M6S 2C8

Editors: Sophie Allen and Hannah Coughlin
Design: Studio Noel
Photography: Helen Fickling*
Production: Lisa Pinnell

*except those listed on page 176

A Cataloguing in Publication record for this title
is available from the British Library

Printed and bound in China

10 9 8 7 6 5 4 3

Plant care key:

☼	full sun
◖	part shade
●	full shade
s	small
M	medium
L	large
✿	flowers
☙	leaves
✿ ☙	both
✓	trouble free
✓✓	requires care
✓✓✓	high maintenance

Introduction

Humans have been living in cities for millennia. From the ancient world onwards, urban settlements have always contained valued areas of greenery for recreation. Today's world is no different. Our large, free public spaces are a huge boon both to local communities and the environment, generating income from tourism and counteracting the smog of pollution. However, as the population of the world increases alarmingly, more and more land is being developed for housing and commerce, which means that opportunities to create new large green spaces are few and far between. Therefore, the green spaces we create for our personal use have become incredibly important not only for ourselves, as we seek private oases in an ever more public world, but also for the wildlife that shares our built-up spaces.

The balance between the human needs for infrastructure and the natural world is a fine one. The small patches of green that individuals create may in themselves appear to amount to nothing. However, combined and taken as a whole, these tiny gardens, roof terraces and balconies form giant patchwork quilts of green that help our cities to breathe.

Designing small city gardens can seem to be a daunting task. How will it be possible to fit all that you wish into such a limited space? What materials should you choose? Which plants will work? Will lighting add an extra dimension to the garden or be a distraction to wildlife? I am asked questions like these by clients on an almost daily basis. Over the past twenty years I have reiterated the same answer: you will be amazed by how much you can fit into a small space with careful planning. Don't be daunted by a small garden's lack of acreage. Instead, be enthused by the challenge of fitting a quart into a pint pot and be aware that by greening up your own urban space you are contributing to a much greater picture.

A bespoke outdoor fireplace warms up a seating area for day or night time use. When not in use the sculptural hood element acts as a focal point at the end of the garden.

Garden design
for small spaces

Making a start

Whether you are starting with a blank canvas or have inherited a previous scheme, making the leap to a new garden design can be challenging, especially with the complications that creating small outside spaces impose. Large gardens have their own issues but compared to intricate and bijou urban spaces they have the enviable luxury of access, scope and scale.

Small gardens are not the poor cousins of the gardening world, though. In fact, I think they are the larger gardens' more complicated yet brilliant relatives. They are clever, innovative, usable spaces that, if designed well, can revolutionise dull, dark courtyards or windy terraces and provide their users with gardens (and yes, they are gardens, even if they are tiny) for year-round enjoyment.

OK, it is clear that I am a fan of small gardens but even I have to admit, as biased as I am, that these tiny spaces do have their issues. Over the years I have dealt with and worked around all manner of challenges in small gardens. Amongst the most common factors are:

- Poor access.
- Issues of privacy and overlooking.
- Tall, bare walls from surrounding buildings and structures.
- Weight restrictions on roof terraces and balconies.

- Shared party walls that can spark arguments between neighbours.
- Limited natural ground to plant into.
- Complicated drainage – this goes for basements as well as roof terraces.
- Air and noise pollution.
- Services on show (AC units, drainpipes, bins) – all of these are visually heightened in a small space.

Perhaps it is best not to think of these criteria as restrictions on your creativity. Instead, think of them as a set of challenges and choices that will assist in refining your thought process and enable you to create a design that will revolutionise the way you use and interact with your outside space.

The modern world bombards us with images and even if you have never undertaken a garden before you may have renovated a property or redecorated rooms. Throughout that process you made a selection of choices based on what you like and what would go with your home; a garden really is no different. If you take your cues from the architecture of your property and its immediate surroundings, with thought and care, you will be amazed by what you can create to fit your plot perfectly, whatever its shape, size, location or elevation.

Previous page: coordinating seating and walling materials in sympathetic tones allows the planting to shine.

Right: strong lines and strong foliage forms create an effect that would be hard to tire of. Keeping it simple is sometimes the answer.

Assessing the site

The first step to designing any garden is to survey the space that you have. Large gardens warrant the services of a survey company, whereas you can usually undertake the survey of a small garden yourself – all you need is a tape measure. A survey will allow you to draw a scaled plan of the garden (you don't need to be an artist, a simple black-and-white scale drawing is all you need), which will enable you to check whether elements will fit into the space or be completely out of scale before you make the decision to buy them or have them delivered to the site. The landscapers' adage of 'measure twice, cut once' is a good rule of thumb to go by.

The second step, in conjunction with the survey, is to assess what you already have to work with. This will help with your design by fine-tuning what is and is not possible. Opposite is a simple set of questions that can be applied to the various types of gardens in this book. Hopefully, they will help to demystify some of the design process and get you well on the way to taking control of your exterior space.

Garden brief: questionnaire

Answering this questionnaire will take you on a journey through the design process and help you make clear decisions. For example, understanding that you only have a 90cm (35in) wide gate and that a crane and road closure will cost you thousands of pounds will reveal that your preferred materials will need to be less than 90cm (35in) wide (ideally less than 80cm (31in) wide if you want to retain the knuckles and fingers on both hands) in order to fit through the gate. There is very little in the design process that is rocket science, but the application of practicality is essential.

Included with the questionnaire are also example answers. I will discuss specific types of gardens later in the book, so for now I have assumed a ground-level landlocked garden.

The questionnaire with sample answers

1. **Which way does the garden face? Is it shady or sunny, protected and still or buffeted by the wind?**
   It is shady and protected at ground level.

2. **Are there any buildings or structures adjacent to or within eyesight of the garden that would be best screened?**
   Yes, there are windows facing into the garden from upper storeys of a building opposite, as well as the blank face of a three-storey-high wall on one side. The rear and side boundaries are fences.

3. **Are there any desirable views that could be incorporated into the scheme?**
   No – none that you would want!

4. **Are there any neighbouring trees that will shed blossom, leaves or fruit into the garden, causing maintenance issues? Will this influence your choice of materials?**
   A large London plane tree overhangs the space, taking up about one quarter of the view to the sky.

5. **How will you use the garden? Is it for relaxing in? Do you need a dining area? Or is the garden just something to be looked at from the house?**
   For dining and relaxing if space allows.

6. **How much gardening do you want to do? Will an irrigation system help?**
   Gentle pottering but little actual gardening. The garden will be left to its own devices for a couple of weeks in the summer and again in the winter, so an irrigation system would be beneficial. My work-life balance also precludes day-to-day watering or care.

7. **Will the garden be seen at all times of the year from the property? Does it need to contain a high percentage of evergreen plants to ensure it looks good in the winter months or can the planting change with the seasons?**
   Yes. There are large glass doors in the back of the property, so the garden is to be considered as part of inside-outside living.

8. **Is the garden accessed via a side entrance or do construction materials and plants need to be carried through a property or lifted onto a roof or into a basement with a crane?**
   All materials will have to be carried through the property.

9. **Should the materials palette be influenced by the interior of the property or is the garden a separate entity in its own right?**
   A link between inside and outside would be the ideal.

10. **Will any allergies, such as asthma, eczema or hay fever, influence your choice of plants?**
    Hay fever brought on by tree pollen early in the year.

What kind of garden would the sample answers generate? The overall style and finishes might vary in the hands of different designers but in essence the scheme would include:

- Materials that are clean and easy to carry through a property (stone or decking would be suitable), with base-up materials in small bags that are easy to manhandle (weighing about 25kg (55lb)).
- Flooring materials that can be easily swept and cleaned and that are tonally or materially the same as the interior finishes of the property to help link the spaces. London plane trees shed large leaves in vast quantities in the autumn – as well as hay fever-inducing pollen and seed-heads in late spring and early summer. There is little that can be done about this as the tree is outside the garden, but making the flooring easy to sweep or hoover (yes, hoovering is an option in a small space) will help to keep ongoing maintenance to a minimum.
- A high percentage of evergreen plants or other plants that hold their structure through the winter. Ideally, 50–70 per cent of the planting would be evergreen. The term 'evergreen' doesn't mean that such plants only have green leaves; *Camellia*, *Rhododendron* and *Nandina* are all evergreens, but they also have the advantage of flowering at different times of the year. The plants selected for this garden will need to be shade tolerant. The overhang of the London plane tree creates a slightly warmer microclimate so hardy tropical plants could even be an option.

- Separate dining and lounging areas. A dining area nearer the property usually makes sense. A lounge area for evening use could be sited somewhere that privacy can be created overhead to make the space inviting and secluded.
- Large pots with feature plants that add high impact but allow easy cleaning around them.
- Something to improve the three-storey wall on the boundary, such as a vertical green wall, backlit decorative filigree panels or simply painting the surface. When affixing items to a wall that is not your property, *always* ask the owner of the wall if it is okay for you to do so.
- Planting to the fence boundaries with simple evergreens that are easy to look after but won't run wild.
- A focal point set on a vista from the property. This could be a water feature, sculpture, decorative planter or architectural plant that could be lit for effect at night.

The layouts opposite show how very different results can be achieved in the same space using the same criteria. Neither is right or wrong. Both work, enhance the garden space and are in tune with the brief. If your garden reflects the brief, you will have achieved what you set out to do. Keep the brief in mind at all times and you won't go wrong. If in doubt, keep it simple. It is far easier to add to a scheme than take elements away from it.

Choosing a design style

Finding your own style

Sometimes the start of the design process can feel intimidating: a blank sheet of paper somehow seems limiting. Using magazines, books, Google and Pinterest for reference and research will result in a never-ending selection of styles and schemes. It is often helpful to cut out or print the things that you like. Once you have half a dozen or so, lay them out together. Are they all of a similar style or are they very different? The likelihood is that they will be relatively similar. You now have a style to work from, even if you didn't know it beforehand. That style can and will influence your design palette and help you to create a layout to which you can apply that palette to bring the garden to life. Sticking to your guns and not being swayed by other images that you come into contact with is important. With that in mind, to follow is some advice on making and using mood boards to keep your design focused.

Creating mood boards to help fine-tune a look and feel for your garden

Visual overload

A quick glance at a magazine shelf in a shop or supermarket will throw up at least fifteen design or gardening magazines in one look. Some magazines concentrate on country homes and gardens whilst others are more urban. Looking through both and pulling out ideas will help you fine-tune a palette for your garden. It might not help you set the definition of the layout, but it will help to fill in some of the blanks as you progress through the design process. You may gravitate towards a colour from a traditional garden but also like the cleaner lines of a more contemporary one or you may look at a colour shown in a bathroom or kitchen photoshoot that sparks an idea in your mind for your garden. Maybe this isn't a wall colour as it is depicted in the magazine but an accent colour or the colour of planting, furniture, fabrics or finishing touches?

Design ideas are everywhere, consider your architecture, visible structures outside of the garden, the vernacular of the area you live in, if it has one, texture and form from fabrics to wood and stone. The apparently endless options can be overwhelming.

A simple solution to this is a mood board – a selection of cuttings from magazines or printed images generated from online searches. Placed all together you might find that you have only picked items that look the same. If so, this is brilliant, and you can move on at pace. Most people – and I include myself in this – will pick a selection of images that they think are going to be right for a space as well as images that fit into a preconceived 'comfort zone'. How often do we opt for

cream walls rather than a bright colour when decorating, just because we know that it is a safe choice?

Refining your mood board by editing out those images that do not fit, whether you love them or not, will help pull a scheme together. If you are still in doubt you can create a separate mood board around the images that you have discarded to see where that process will take you and you will then have (hopefully) two distinctly different styles that you can choose from. Even if one style falls into your 'comfort zone' it may well be the one to opt for, after all, you will be expending time and money on your new garden and you will want it to be something that you will love for many years to come. If your backdrop is neutral, then you can always change up your furniture and pots to update the scheme in years to come.

The example mood boards (left) show the process of refinement detailed above. From one set of cuttings two distinct styles are created, all from images that I like. There are some images that have had to be ruthlessly culled, even if they are stunning, as they may be unachievable in terms of scale and budget. As with all small garden spaces, with their notoriously poor access, large-format items, which admittedly always work to make a space look bigger (and always look enticingly fabulous in magazines) sometimes have to be omitted or scaled back because they just will not fit through or over a property.

If once you have put your mood boards together you are still unclear on mixing materials, there are a couple of ways to consider this:

1. Complementary materials

These materials will be tonally similar; think cream stone flooring, light-coloured walls, softly coloured terracotta pots.

Complementary schemes

Option A

- New-sawn natural stone.
- Natural wood or artificial timber in a light colour.
- Fencing in a colour to match the decking.
- Polished pebbles.
- Real lawn.
- A simple bowl water feature in a cream colour.
- Light terracotta planters in varying shapes and sizes for herbs and annuals.
- Textured, soft pretty planting in pastel shades.

Option B

- Grey limestone or Basalt paving or setts.
- Dark grey clay pavers.
- Dark grey painted fencing.
- Matt grey pebbles.
- Artificial lawn.
- Polished Basalt cube water feature.
- Regimented same-size planters with clipped green forms in them.
- Bold textured foliage in shades of green.

The above schemes illustrate how light and dark can work in the garden and how different materials can change up a scheme. Option A would create a light, bright effect with a soft feel and would make the garden feel larger. Option B is more dynamic and demanding on the eye and would draw the garden in, making it feel much more intimate, even though the palette is still a complementary one.

2. Contrasting materials

These do not need to clash and be visually jarring, but they will have more of a colour contrast than complementary materials; grey paving, natural timber fencing, metal (rusted or polished), steel are also all natural but the difference in the shade and texture makes them more of a statement within a scheme.

Sample palettes are helpful so below is a list of possible options for colour and material selections. It is by no means complete or comprehensive – that would be a book or two on its own:

Contrasting schemes

Option A

- Dutch clay pavers or bricks.
- Natural wood decking or artificial wood in a mid or dark wood tone.
- Fencing in a colour to match the decking.
- Matt pebbles.
- Real lawn.
- A simple bowl water feature in a Corten steel.
- Textured concrete details/walls with structured evergreen.
- A mix of topiary forms and grasses as well as overhead multi-stem trees.

Option B

- Grey natural stone paving (smooth or riven).
- Light clay pavers or bricks.
- Corten steel fencing.
- Polished black pebbles.
- Decorative aggregate instead of lawn.
- Decorative water feature.
- Painted wooden planters.
- A simple planting palette of Bamboo and grasses.

These contrasting schemes allow for light and shade within a scheme and are more visually demanding than complementary ones. That said, they often create more successful gardens, especially in small spaces where drama is required to make up for a lack of scale.

Whichever option you decide upon should be based upon your personal taste and the look and feel of your home, especially if your garden is going to be seen as a true extension of your living space.

Garden types

Basement gardens

There is nothing quite like starting with a challenge, and basement gardens are certainly one of the most challenging of all city spaces to fill. Generally dark and overlooked, often with no natural ground and lacking in adequate drainage, basements absolutely impose a set of design do's and don'ts.

Every successful garden design, no matter where, needs to be tailored to its site and situation, and none more so than a basement garden. That said, basement gardens can be charming spaces that totally transform the ground they sit on from grotty concrete box to lush green oasis. Don't think of basement gardens as one-dimensional, though. Such gardens can be looked into and also looked down upon, so a simple design, well laid out and defined with planting that has an attractive canopy and strong backbone, is advisable. Whether your preferred garden style is abundant and tropical or stylised and minimal, the chances are that you will be creating greenery where there was none before. The benefit of this starting situation is that a blank canvas is always the easiest to work from.

Out of all urban gardens, basements devoid of greenery are the least likely to interact with or entice wildlife. Landlocked by masonry and generally a vertical storey below ground level, basement gardens are not wildly attractive habitats for wildlife, perhaps with the exception of woodlice and spiders, who seem to consider any nook and cranny to be a home. On the plus side, you may never see a slug or snail, even after you have planted the garden, unless they brave the traverse across road and pavement, which is not unheard of. You will see an increase in bees and other pollinating insects almost immediately after your garden is completed; and birds will follow swiftly after that. Greening even the smallest of city spaces in the tiniest of ways can have a beneficial impact upon the environment.

Previous page: an industrial style scheme crafted from recycled materials and dark paving is softened by planting at all levels, even under the table with shade lovers.

Right: emphasising the 'inside/outside' effect, steps on the inside are echoed outside with planting in terraces to minimise the impact of the changes in level between basement and ground floor.

Following page: showcasing semi tropical species in a frost-free environment, this garden demonstrates how even dark spaces can be transformed with the right materials and planting.

The do's

Simple, bold, strong – these are the keys to transforming a small dark basement into a year round garden that can be easily maintained and therefore enjoyed at your leisure.

Do be bold with your design. A strong and simple design will always work better than something complicated.

Do select elements that will extend the use of the garden. Assessing at what times of the year you will use your garden will greatly assist the design process, ensuring that you can include all of the elements that will make it function for you and your needs.

Do use light-reflecting materials. Light and space – two words that go hand in hand. There is nothing like light be it natural sunshine or even artificial light at night to enhance a small space making it feel brighter, larger and more dynamic.

Do minimise your plant palette. Less can very much be more. Less maintenance, more impact and drama. In a busy world, small bold gardens often look the best for longer throughout the year.

Do consider planting under steps and changes of level. In small compact spaces, any extra greening you create will always make the garden feel more welcoming and with a high percentage of evergreens keep it looking great all year round.

Be bold with your design

- A strong and simple design will always work better than something complicated. More often than not, straight lines (rather than curves) will make a small space feel larger. Throw out some 45-degree lines to encourage the eye to the corners of the space.
- Try building in furniture around the perimeter of the space rather than using stand-alone elements in the centre. This will allow you to create integrated storage solutions for cushions and small gardening tools on the boundaries, while keeping the centre of the space open and more flexible.
- Supersize your pots and troughs. Use one large planter rather than a group of pots to create impact. This will ensure that the space remains uncluttered but still has drama. One planter is less to water and maintain, too. The only caveat to this advice is to make sure that whatever you select will fit through the access to your garden.

Select elements that will extend the use of the garden

- If you are able to use the garden only in the evenings or at the weekend, fine-tune elements to ensure the space is as enticing as possible. Create or purchase furniture that can be left outside year-round. If you need to add cushions, make sure there is somewhere dry nearby in which to store them, or have waterproof furniture covers made to fit. Furniture covers aren't expensive and will prolong the life of any soft furnishings kept outside where the elements can be cruel.
- Add a barbecue or fire-pit for entertaining. Sitting around a fire at the end of the day (be it natural gas, wood or bioethanol) can be very calming, as well as warming on a chilly but dry evening. All exterior fires have their pros and cons so do your research before purchasing. If you cannot channel natural gas to the space, bioethanol may be the best solution for you.
- Consider an automated awning – not for shade but for privacy – that can be deployed without diminishing light levels inside the property. Many awnings contain both lighting and heating, which is a bit of a double whammy bonus in a small space.

- Although slightly controversial, exterior speakers, if used discreetly, can add a whole new dimension to an exterior space, making it far more interactive and inviting. It should go without saying, I hope, that if you like your music loud, do consider your neighbours and keep the volume down!
- Add lighting. Always be mindful of your neighbours, though. Avoid lights that shine directly skywards.

Use light-reflecting materials

- Light-coloured stone or porcelain tiles in large-format sizes can really help a small area feel more generous. Porcelain has come a long way in recent years, and there are now many options that look as good as natural stone but are much easier to clean – a key consideration for spaces that catch the dirt easily, such as basements.
- Mirror-polished stainless-steel and mirrors have the ability to bounce light around and also create illusions of space. They should be sited with planting surrounding them. Do not situate them anywhere that birds could mistake the reflections for air and fly into them. Truly reflective surfaces demand ongoing care (if they become dirty or marked the illusion is destroyed), so avoid them if you are after a very low-maintenance scheme.
- If the boundary walls are sound and dry, render and paint the wall or simply paint it with a pale-coloured exterior masonry paint or clad it with a pale stone affixed with exterior adhesive. You will be amazed at the proportion-enhancing qualities that a coat of white paint can do to the size of a basement garden.
- Planters come in many different shapes, sizes, colours and forms. There are mirror-polished stainless-steel ones, shiny ceramic ones, concrete, terracotta and powder-coated ones, to name but a few. Like mirrors, any planters intended to look crisp and clean will require a wash down regularly to keep their lustre, so they aren't for the maintenance shy or those pressed for time. If you are happy with a less perfect finish, then terracotta and textured concrete are certainly viable options instead.

Minimise your plant palette

- Quite simply, less can very much be more. Always select plants that will thrive in the conditions. An evergreen backbone is essential for your scheme but do not discount colour as well. All the plants you select must be happy when grown in containers.
- Topiary – *Taxus* is less problematic than *Buxus* and *Laurus nobilis*/Bay tree will cope with a degree more shade than its Mediterranean roots suggest.
- *Dicksonia antarctica* (tree fern) and herbaceous ferns look wonderful in sheltered basement gardens and require little care. Admittedly these only exhibit green foliage with no showy flowers, but the range of greens from dark to acid green and even silver as well as some of the best-textured foliage the plant world has to offer makes them invaluable choices for small shady gardens.
- Trouble-free small shrubs such as half-standard, grafted *Acer* varieties, *Sarcococca* (Christmas box) and *Skimmia* might not set the world alight with colourful summer displays but they are good shade-tolerant stalwarts. The framework of the *Acer* is interesting, even when bare in the winter, and it can be underplanted with bulbs. The *Sarcococca* and *Skimmia* both flower in the winter and their sweet scents will enliven any small space when there is little else of interest in flower. Many evergreens have glossy leaves and the *Sarcococca* and *Skimmia* are no exception, making them useful additions not just for their year-round appeal but also because they add life to a scheme.
- Adding colour will create seasonality in a basement garden and give it a connection to the wider landscape. *Hydrangea*, *Paeonia*, *Helleborus* and even some varieties of roses will cope with a degree of shade and containerisation if sited correctly. To thrive, though, they must be planted in the appropriate soil and fed, not just when planted but yearly.
- All container-grown plants require more care than they would if grown in the ground. Their lifespan will be reduced unless you can repot them into larger planters over time. You may prefer to donate any plants that have outgrown their planters to friends and family and choose something new to grow in their place.

- If you like green as a colour, then you are in luck. The most successful small, shady basement spaces contain multiple shades of green, including ferns, *Hosta*, *Fatsia*, bamboo varieties and, if you live in an enviable frost-free location, you could even try *Aspidistra*, *Philodendron* and *Schefflera* for a more exotic feel. Generally, evergreen plants are less messy than deciduous ones, with the exception of bamboo. This statuesque plant has many good qualities but it is without doubt a very generous 'leaf shedder'. It loses its old leaves as the new ones emerge in the summer and the fallen leaves with their narrow form have an unerring ability to embed themselves everywhere – always just slightly out of reach of a broom. If you have a little more space than a tiny basement plot and like sweeping, bamboo may be the plant for you, otherwise give them a wide berth!

Consider planting under steps and changes of level

- Steps can be constructed from a multitude of different materials, some of which are made to feel lighter and less obvious in small spaces with open treads and/or risers. If you garden in a basement you may well have to work around either a fire escape or an access route that's in daily use. Although often overlooked as purely utilitarian, it is possible in some cases to under-plant steps with ferns and shade-tolerant perennials to create a much softer overall feel.
- If there is no natural ground to plant in to (and there may well not be in a basement), then potting up a selection of planters or long troughs can also work very well. As stand-alone items that can be easily moved around you are then also free to ring the changes any time you want to freshen up your scheme.

The don'ts

As you read through this book you will learn that I am not a great believer in design having to be right for the sake of design alone. If a layout works for you and isn't 'designery' then it works as a design because it works for you. It would be rather dull and bland if we all liked the same thing and looked the same way. That said, there are some things that should not be included in small basement gardens. Thankfully, the list is short and refers more to practicality than personal taste.

Don't use very dark colours, they will make a small space feel oppressive, small and rather depressing.

Don't increase the heights of the surrounding walls with trellis unless you absolutely crave anonymity – standing in the garden will feel like being at the bottom of a bunker.

Don't plant Mediterranean or tropical sun-loving plants. It goes without saying in all gardens that it should always be 'right plant, right place', and basement gardens are absolutely no exception to this rule.

Don't use too much bling if you are trying to create areas of 'shine' with light-reflecting materials. Try to use these elements as highlights, contrasting them with more textured finishes, otherwise you will spend your precious downtime polishing your garden – and there is much more to life than that.

Plants for basement gardens

How many plants should you select? If you had the room, you could add all of the plants suggested on the following pages to your scheme; they would all work well together. However, we are talking about designing for small spaces so a refined selection of plants would work best. You need to be able to dilute all that you want into perhaps just half a dozen plants. This can be a challenging concept for gardeners. After all, we garden because we love growing plants. For a small garden, you need plants to give your design an evergreen backbone, plus colour at some times of the year to mark the seasons and perhaps provide some scent. Carefully selecting the plants for your precious space will mean that you have a scheme and palette that is easy to care for and should thrive for years to come. The hard choice is deciding which plants you will use.

When space, light and access conspire against you and there is no way to get water to a landlocked courtyard – consider artificial. Sometimes there is a time and a place for greening without real plants.

Alocasia varieties

Warm season growers which may require winter protection, even in a sheltered basement garden, but it is worth the care for its amazing leaves and structure. Make sure it doesn't dry out though, and team with *Hosta* or ferns for a totally tropical look.

● M&L ✿ ✓✓✓

Aspidistra elatior

Yes, this is the much-loved plant of Victorian parlours that gets its common name of 'cast iron plant' from its cast iron constitution. It is tough, almost un-killable, and hardier than you might think. If you garden reliably frost free, try it outside where it will most probably surprise you with its tolerance to deep shade and some neglect.

◖● M&L ✿ ✓✓✓

Begonia rex varieties

These are the multi coloured leafy types, not the heavy bloomed hanging basket types. Hues of purple, silver, metallic pewter and pink, as well as a kaleidoscope of greens (often all in one leaf), make these an acquired taste, but they certainly pack a visual punch and you will be amazed at how much weather and shade they can take.

◖● S ✿✿ ✓

Camellia sasanqua

If there is a plant that looks too fragile to be able to flower through the winter then *Camellia sasanqua* is it. Papery blooms crinkle and brown at the mere threat of frost, if sheltered and frost free then this steady shrub will flower all winter. Like the *Rhododendron*, ericaceous soil is a must.

◖● M&L ✿✿ ✓

Dicksonia antarctica

Akin to herbaceous ferns but with huge fronds elevated on a hairy trunk. Planted at jaunty angles in the ground or in pots, they are eye-catching from all directions. In sheltered town gardens they may hold their leaves all year, but in frost prone areas protect with straw or horticultural fleece in the winter. Remember to water from the top.

◖● M&L ✿ ✓✓

Fatsia japonica

King of the evergreens, this large shrub with palmate shiny foliage takes hard pruning well, making it viable for container gardening. Bobbly white flowers turn into jet black berries in the winter. A plant that doesn't really need companion planting, but if you prefer to hide the top of the pot you could plant with hardy *Begonia* or *Soleirolia* underneath.

◖● L ✿✿ ✓

Helleborus varieties

Winter would not be winter without Hellebores. Whether you pick the single or double flowered forms they will bring a smile to your face on the dullest of days. Braving the worst of the weather, these plants work well with other winter bloomers such as *Galanthus* (Snowdrops) and later in the year with lighter perennials such as *Tiarella* and *Anthriscus*.

☼◖● S ✿✿ ✓

Herbaceous ferns

These are my 'go to' plants for shady spaces and they add drama and texture. Ferns can equally play the leading role centre stage or take a bit part at the rear of a border. Use single specimens in large planters where they require little care, save for a removal of dead fronds in the spring and an assurance of regular water.

◖● S, M&L ✿ ✓

Hosta varieties

An epic foliage plant that rockets out of the ground in the spring, pushing up pointed black shoots which unfurl into fabulous textural leaves, these are topped in summer with elegant sprays of white or lilac blooms (some varieties are also scented). If slugs and snails are your nemesis, do use a biological control to keep them in check.

☼◖● S&M ✿✿ ✓

Hydrangea 'Bombshell'

Most *Hydrangea* are too large for small basement gardens, but this variety tops out at about 1m (3ft) and so makes it an ideal candidate, especially if you're after summer colour. It will be very unhappy if it dries out, so ensure it is well watered and combine with *Hosta* and ferns for a paired down, timeless scheme.

Hydrangea seemannii

An evergreen self-clinging climbing *Hydrangea* that although admittedly painfully slow growing, is well worth the time and effort. Your patience will be rewarded with elegant white blooms like horticultural fascinator hats in the summer. Keep an eye out for vine weevil and treat with a biological control.

Philodendron xanadu

A houseplant that will cope with the shelter and micro climate afforded by shaded town gardens. Perhaps it wont reach the dizzying heights it could inside a glasshouse, but its tropical dark green shiny leaves are a strong foil to lighter plants and ferns. It is certainly a plant to try out, especially in tropical schemes.

Phyllostachys varieties

Bamboo, a plant that generates 'Marmite-like' reactions. There are those that love it and those that hate it. I am a lover although I hate the mess it makes. Try cleaning the first 1–1.5m (3–5ft) of stem of leaves, mulch underneath with pebbles and ensure a regular supply of water during growth to minimise leaf drop and scorching.

Rhododendron yakushimanum

These are useful evergreens in the *Rhododendron* family that generally do not exceed 1–1.5m (3–5ft) and settle well into containers, provided they are planted in ericaceous soil. Pale and pastel flowers add interest in early summer. These are best as single specimens if you do not have the room to group them in natural soil beds.

Sarcococca confusa

Christmas Box, also known as Sweet Box, definitely lives up to its name. In the winter its spicy scent can be appreciated from metres away and its small shiny leaves reflect light and add interest at other times of the year. It is a perfect foil for lower growing perennials as well as *Digitalis* (Foxgloves).

Skimmia japonica

A quiet plant that you may not even notice until it buds up in late winter. Tiny little tight balls explode into to star shaped flowers that have a wonderful sweet scent. Often used in winter containers as a 'bedding' plant but you can pot these on after flowering and grow them into full sized shrubs, best planted in semi-shade.

Tiarella varieties

Tiarella produce a mass of foamy pink flowers for simply ages in the spring and summer, with lovely bright green, often mottled leaves underneath. These can look OK on their own but are best planted en-masse. Under-plant with *Scilla* or *Muscari* for a pretty spring show or combine with ferns and *Epimedium* in more shaded locations.

Trachelospermum jasminoides

This is a useful and well-mannered climbing plant with shiny oval leaves and wonderfully fragrant star shaped white flowers, borne in mid-summer. Although it will suffer a degree of shade, it flowers best in full sun where it will soon clothe boundaries in its rich green sheen.

Small urban gardens and courtyards

Designing a small urban garden or courtyard is a luxury. (I don't mean that it comes with a gold-edged price tag, rather I'm referring to the amount of space you have to play with.) They are just that little bit bigger than a basement garden and allow a tiny bit more scope for a design to really take shape. Of all of the garden spaces available to green, they are probably the most generous and have the fewest problems associated with plant choice, access and materials. They are also the most encouraging for wildlife. It only takes a few simple steps to create wildlife habitats, corridors and feeding stations that have little bearing on the human use of the garden but aid the environmental balance hugely. Surely it is far better to encourage hedgehogs to consume and control slugs and snails than it is to pour chemicals and pellets onto the ground? A simple bird feeder might entice squirrels (the scourge of tulip bulbs) but it will also encourage flocks of birds that will help to decimate the local aphid population while also giving you the joy of watching them flit about.

Slightly larger gardens can, of course, contain more elements than tiny basement gardens, but those elements still have to work hard. Whether you are creating a garden for a young family, a single user, a professional couple or retirees, successful small gardens must contain all the components that make modern interaction with the garden possible – and that doesn't necessarily mean the plants. Living an 'inside-outside' lifestyle – or aspiring to that way of life in a somewhat soggy climate – requires hard surfaces for dining and lounging, space for children to play safely, areas for quiet relaxation as well as those for entertaining. Shoehorning all of these requirements into a small space without it feeling cluttered is possible (with perhaps a little editing). However, it is not always possible to do this on a tight budget.

Large gardens are fortunate to have areas of lawn, which are by far the least expensive surface to implement in a garden. Once you enter the realms of paving, decking, walls, built structures with retaining walls and trellis, costs escalate. If your budget doesn't allow for the creation of an entire garden in one go, then it is easiest to create your small space in stages – just make sure you start from the furthest point from the house and work backwards, otherwise you will need to traipse over work you have already completed – and there is nothing more soul-destroying than that.

Ensuring that your design is bold will give it longevity and make it appealing for as much of the year as possible. Get the bones of the scheme right and the planting will shine.

———

'There should always be a harmonious balance between hard and soft landscaping in a garden.'

———

It takes very little to make me happy; knowing that a garden has adequate access is sufficient. If a property has a side entrance that is large enough for a wheelbarrow — or, even better, a small digger — then the design process can be far less inhibited by the access issues that constrain basement gardens and roof terraces. That being said, there should always be a harmonious balance between hard and soft landscaping in a garden scheme. Neither should dominate. Sometimes that can feel difficult to achieve if the wish list for the space contains the following: barbecue or outdoor kitchen; shed and storage spaces; terrace or decking; children's play area; lawn; lighting; hot tub; privacy (for example, you don't want to see your neighbours and you don't want them to see you).

With a wish list as long as your arm, where do you start? Will curves work or should the scheme be angular? Well, with the little bit of extra ground that these types of garden afford, you can do both. Some people gravitate to the angular and others prefer softer lines. Either way, the same principles for designing a garden apply: measure twice, cut once.

A scaled plan is vital. I may sound like a broken record but this is important because it will allow you to quantify the amount of materials you require and also help you see how the layout works and what furniture, planters and finishing touches will fit.

While basement gardens are, in the main, created with materials carried through the property, small gardens have a little more scope, though you still may have to consider buying flat-pack elements that can be constructed in situ rather than pre-assembled items.

So with more space and more scope, are there any specific design do's and don'ts for small urban gardens and courtyards? Yes, is the short answer, though they are far fewer and they are less restrictive than those for basement gardens.

What small gardens lack in volume, they can more than make up for with dramatic planting. Architectural forms work really well and are often relatively low maintenance.

45

The do's

Maintain the vision for your space at all times. Keeping this in mind and not deviating from it (within the realms of a creative process of course) will ensure that your finished garden is exactly what you had in mind.

Do set a budget. The larger the space the easier it is for the budget to escalate. As with building, much of the costs of a landscaping project are sub surface. Just because foundations cannot be seen doesn't mean they should be scrimped on.

Do decide on the scope. Deciding upon and creating a layout for your scheme is important. Sticking to it through the implementation process is vital to keep a handle on your budget.

Do refine your wish list. Review the items on your wish list and select only those elements that you really want and need. It is important to be realistic.

Do consider lighting for practical use and entertainment. Lighting extends the use of your garden as well as creating a beautiful and inviting outlook.

Do evaluate your site's soil and aspect. This will help your choices when it comes to choosing plants, ensuring you pick the right plant for the right place in your garden.

Do get to know your neighbours. Communication is the key, and keeping on the right side of neighbours whilst building a garden will ensure a far happier outcome for all, especially when you start using your new outdoor space.

———

'Taking your time when choosing pots, furniture and art will allow you to really evaluate what you want, need and like'

———

Set a budget
- A spreadsheet sounds very 'design limiting', but a full schedule of costs as you progress through a project will be so helpful with managing the final figures. It will also assist with what can be achieved when, and whether finishing touches such as furniture, which can be costly, will have to wait for another season.

Decide on the scope
- Where will your terraces be sited? Will these be in the sun or the shade? If they are in the sun, will you need to provide shade to allow for dining or sitting in the afternoon? If they are in the shade, will some additional heating be required to make them more enticing places in which to spend time? Do they have to be linked or can areas of lawn or stepping stones separate them?

Left: contrasting materials and textures can make a space feel larger. Dark materials work especially well with velvety plum tones and lots of greens.

Following page: areas of light and shade can transform a garden, creating an enticing space to spend time in at the end of the day.

- How large will these areas be? Will the amount of entertaining you do or the number of people you want to seat at any single time influence this?
- Do you want to hide a children's play area or should it be on full view in case of accidents?

Refine your wish list
- A hot tub or swimming pool, for example, are aspirational items. Will they fit in the space you have and still leave room for all of the other things that you want as well? Will they blow the budget before you have even begun?
- Can the elements be added gradually? Taking your time to select pots, furniture and art will allow you to really evaluate what you want, need and like. It may also allow you to make your purchases at the most economical time of year.
- Do all the elements you like go together? There is no hard-and-fast rule for this. In a small space that is often viewed in one glance, limiting the palette of finishing touches to a tonal range or selecting one thing as a highlight will create a much more calming effect than multiple features that catch your eye all over the design.

——

'Limiting your palette to a tonal range or selecting one finishing touch as a highlight will create a much more calming effect.'

——

Consider lighting for practical use and entertainment

- Lighting is a revolutionary way to extend the use of your garden. Returning home after spending long hours at work, the simple flick of a switch can bring your garden to life.
- Electric lights are the most flexible way to illuminate your garden but you could also consider candles. They might not be as user-friendly, but they do provide a lovely soft light with a gentle movement that is wonderfully relaxing. Citronella ones can help to minimise biting insects.

Evaluate your site's soil and aspect

- Selecting plants is both hugely enjoyable and also mind-boggling. So how can you limit the endless possibilities? Assessment of your site and, more importantly, soil will ease this dilemma. Is your soil:
  - a) Heavy clay: Claggy and wet in the winter and dry in the summer. Very high in nutrients.
  - b) Sandy: Light and dry with little structure and poor nutrients. Often acidic.
  - c) Silt: Fertile and very fine. Susceptible to compaction due to its wet nature.
  - d) Loam: A combination of all the above with the best qualities of each. In essence, the ideal soil type. Sadly, it is a rarity in towns and cities.
- Work out the path of the sun throughout the day. Which parts of the garden are the sunniest? Which are the shadiest?
- Are any parts of the garden in a rain shadow (sheltered from the prevailing rain by a wall, tree or large shrubs, for example) or in the full blast of wind funnelled down a side entrance or through a gap?
- Which elements in the garden do you wish to retain, if any? Many trees in urban gardens have Tree Preservation Orders (TPOs) applied to them, which means you will not be able to prune or fell them without submitting an application for approval. Any illegal work on trees with a TPO carries a hefty fine. TPOs aside, trees add maturity to a scheme and are always something that I will fight vehemently to retain, not only because they are wonderful habitats for wildlife but also because they provide shade, screening, privacy and change wonderfully with the seasons.

Get to know your neighbours

- New homeowners who change an old garden to suit their tastes can, and often do, generate neighbourly disputes.
- Take the time to explain any plans to your neighbours. If there is going to be noise or mess, discuss this with them in advance: forewarned is forearmed.
- Always discuss any changes to trellis or boundary walls.
- Above all, be respectful – you do not want to start a war over a garden.

Following page: two wall lights shine down washing a dining table set for an evening meal in a flattering light. A dramatic effect that also keeps light pollution to a minimum.

The don'ts

One of the easiest ways to deviate from a budget is with changes to a design. Along with the financial burden this causes, changing and diluting the design often results in a garden that isn't as great as it would have been if the original plan was followed. Sometimes you have to be brave to create something wonderful.

Don't throw the kitchen sink at your design. Keep it simple, usable and practical.

Don't assume costs won't escalate. There are always 'unknowns' when building any garden. Make sure you set your costs in advance and try to stick to them. Also ensure you have some contingency for the unexpected (10% is a sensible amount).

Don't create a water feature unless you really have the time to look after it. They are undoubtedly lovely elements, adding a wonderful dimension and sensory experience to a garden, but they are high maintenance and without ongoing care and adequate filtration they will turn to green gloop in the blink of an eye.

Don't use materials that are totally out of keeping with your property and the surrounding area.

Don't plant anything that will outgrow its space quickly and overtake any underplanting you have considered.

Don't pave under trees. This is a bit of a no-brainer. Paving under trees will be unsuccessful on several fronts: tree roots will lift paving and decking (although decking is doable under a tree with a light canopy); any birds roosting or perching in the tree will leave 'unmentionable' splodges on any hard surface below that will stain; and, most importantly, you will suffocate the tree.

Do's and don'ts are never hard-and-fast rules. What works for one person and one site may not work for another. Tailor your small garden or courtyard specifically to your needs and the amount of time and dedication you have for the upkeep of your space, and it will be all the more successful for it.

Design options for a tight budget – Although many of the elements required to create a garden are not expensive (such as a bag of sand or a single plant), when you combine everything needed to create a space that is probably the 'biggest room in your home' as well as including labour costs (if you are not heading down the DIY route) costs will soon clock up. Due to the extra land in small gardens it is worth keeping in mind the following if you are on a tight budget:

- A lawn is a relatively inexpensive form of ground cover. If your garden has good light and full sun and you'd prefer an option that requires less maintenance, consider planting a thyme or chamomile lawn. Bees and insects will thank you for this. Although it won't need to be mown weekly, a herb lawn will have its own special maintenance requirements.
- Fences and boundaries can be greened. Doing this will result in a generous space that feels welcoming, defined and protected. Fast-growing climbers, wall-trained shrubs and – expensive but instant – vertical green walls will clothe boundaries and encourage wildlife.
- Paving and hard surfaces do not have to be brand new. Contemporary schemes warrant new stone and wood but softer, more traditional layouts will benefit from recycled, preloved or upcycled materials.

Not every material used has to be new. Think outside the box, scaffold boards and expanded mesh are not expensive but used well can create a strong effect to which a foliage rich planting palette responds well.

Plants for small urban gardens and courtyards

The slightly larger scope of these gardens increases the number of potential plants that could be used. Therefore, the following lists are split into architectural forms and softer, more colourful planting. These distinct styles allow the creation of strong gardens – those that will work all year round. There is absolutely no reason why you cannot 'mix and match' these plants between their styles to create your own unique garden. Referring back to your original mood board and adding in the plants you have selected will help you decide whether these plants work together, as well as suit the style and look you are hoping to achieve. This is an inexpensive way of putting a planting scheme in place and ensuring you stick to your original vision.

Sometimes it is a bold step to go 'bold', but it can work with incredible results if done correctly.

Plants with architectural form

Architectural plants undeniably add drama; leaves, stems, and form combined together making a strong statement. They work on all scales, from large country estates to tiny town gardens. Their ability to transform a space, often simply by a single presence, is highlighted in small gardens, though, where their leaves add interest and shadow during the day and create nothing short of 'ooomph' at night, especially when pared with lighting. These plants are the perfect exponent of 'less is more'; a single *Fatsia*, *Dicksonia*, *Astelia*, or even topiary form in a planter can do so much more for a small space than a group of less impressive specimens. This may feel like 'placing' rather than 'gardening', but if you are time pressured then they certainly add impact without hours of maintenance.

Natural stone materials, in their many textures and colours, can create soft backdrops for architectural plants, despite their hard nature.

Acer varieties

Japanese Maples are beautifully clothed in delicate red or green leaves in summer which turn fiery in autumn. Plant in semi shade away from desiccating winds, either on their own or with a carpet of plants such as Hosta or ferns. Ensure regular water in the growing season if containerised.

◗ M & L ❀ ✓

Euphorbia mellifera

The Honey Spurge lives up to its common name with bronze flowers emitting a sweet scent in summer. A plant with presence and a fast grower to boot, covered in whorled shiny semi-evergreen leaves, you will probably only need one. When stems are cut the sap can burn skin, so wear gloves when pruning.

☼ M & L ❀❧ ✓

Nandina domestica varieties

Elegant evergreen plum flushed green leaves with sprays of pretty pale pink flowers and coral berries. This is one very hard-working plant that behaves as impeccably in the garden as it does in a container. Pair with large leaved plants for contrast.

☼◗ M & L ❀❧ ✓

Phyllostachys

There are many forms of bamboo, but Phyllostachys are the most available. Although generally easy to grow, their arch nemesis is a lack of water upon which the leaves will brown, crisp and drop from the plant quickly. If well-watered and fed the reward is a wonderful year-round display that adds impact.

☼◗ M & L ❧ ✓

Multi-stem trees

Natural form trees reflect the current less rigid trend in garden design. Used in pairs they can also give a formal look. Deciduous varieties include Amelanchier, Betula alba, Cornus kousa, Prunus serrula, and Syringa meyeri, and evergreen ones include Buxus sempervirens, Olea europaea and Pinus varieties.

☼◗ M & L ❀❧ ✓

Ilex crenata bonsai

Aspirational plants for large planters or Oriental gardens. Although a member of the tough Holly family, Ilex crenata require specific care and a growth spurt in the summer may result in two trims a year. Feed appropriately to avoid yellow leaves. If in doubt, consult the supplier for ongoing care.

☼ M & L ❧ ✓

Osmanthus fragrans

Often trained into a multi-stem specimen, these have reliably evergreen foliage above interesting stems that allow blousy, soft under-planting to great effect. A simple up-light underneath turns them from plant to sculpture at night. Generally trouble-free, they work well either in the ground or large planters.

☼ M & L ❀❧ ✓

Taxus and other topiary

Yew, Buxus (pictured) and Ilex are tough plants. They can grow into large trees but are equally happy clipped into hedges or shapes. Their green forms add punctuation to lighter planting schemes and can be both traditional and contemporary in feel. Classical plants that transcend taste and time effortlessly.

☼◗● S, M & L ❧ ✓

Astelia chathamica

A native of New Zealand, with downy iridescent silvery spear-like leaves, similar in form to Phormium. Can tolerate semi shade and are of huge benefit to a winter scheme where the evergreen foliage shines. They prefer a moisture rich soil, but not overly wet, so drainage should be improved if on heavy clay.

☼◗ M ❧ ✓

Melianthus major

Silver serrated (oddly scented) leaves elegantly clothe this fast grower in full sun. It is equally happy in semi shade where growth is slightly curtailed. Pair with Geum or Salvia in sun and ferns or Liriope in shade. A cold, wet winter could mark its demise, but if sheltered this is unlikely, unless it becomes waterlogged.

☼◗ M & L ❀❧ ✓

Phormium varieties

These sword-like evergreen leaves have been bred for colour. The less vigorous variegated forms are most suited to small spaces. Primordial flower spikes erupting in the summer are an added bonus. They require little care, only the removal of tatty leaves in spring, making them perfect for the time limited gardener.

☼◗ M & L ❀❧ ✓

Trachycarpus fortunei and Chamaerops humilis

Hardy palms are ideal for frost-free locations, but can cope with some cold. Bold and architectural, they are best in full sun but sheltered so that wind cannot shred the leaves. Fairly trouble free, these statuesque evergreens are a perfect backbone for dramatic gardens.

☼ M & L ❧ ✓

Plants with softer form

Every garden needs a degree of structure, be that in evergreen form, clipped formality or even grasses, but these alone (even the grasses) impose a regimented feel to a space. The creation of a garden that works across the seasons with colourful highlights requires a lighter palette. It certainly doesn't all have to be soft, but the harmonious balance of structure and colour is one that gardeners have been deploying for millennia, so there must be something of value in it!

Ethereal planting provides a light and airy effect which contrasts strong vertical hard landscaping. Shadows are thrown onto walls and add an extra dimension to the scheme.

Astrantia varieties

Best planted in groups in the ground, not containers. Pin-cushion blooms appear in the summer and last for weeks, often with a second flush after dead-heading. Best in sun or very light shade. Shades of white and pink combine well with small *Euphorbia*, *Anemone* and ornamental grasses.

☼◖ S ✿ ✓✓✓

Agapanthus varieties

Given a few simple ingredients, Agapanthus put on a spectacular summer display with single plants of 30–40 flowers. Ensuring a generous supply of water when in growth is vital and if you can, liquid feed in the summer, the rewards will be worth it. Agapanthus will grow and bloom very happily in a large planter.

● S & M ✿ ✓✓

Allium

The ornamental Onion in shades of purple, white and blue is much used at The Chelsea Flower Show as they reliably start to bloom in late spring. Mixing varieties prolongs interest through the summer and old flowerheads look wonderful in a winter scheme with ornamental grasses.

☼ S & M ✿ ✓

Clematis varieties

A vast family comprising many different forms; nodding bells, simple four petalled flowers, open dinner plate sized blooms and tiny stars. Most are unscented but those that do smell have a far-reaching aroma. Always follow horticultural directions, especially relating to the depth of planting, to avoid *Clematis* wilt.

☼◖ S & M ✿ ✓✓

Euphorbia varieties

From tiny ground hugging forms to giant sub shrubs, the *Euphorbia* family is both interesting and varied. Consider the varieties *E.characias*, *E. x martini* and *E. amygdaloides*. Most prefer sun but, for rampant evergreen ground cover in shade *E. amygdaloides* is the plant for you. Wear gloves when handling.

☼◖ S, M & L ✿▲ ✓✓

Geranium varieties

One of the best do-ers in the plant world. Tough and generally no-nonsense, they do not require a great deal of intervention. There are Geranium for sun, shade, hot dry, cold and wet. Ensure you select one that suits your site; they give so much and demand so little it would be hard to garden without them.

☼◖● S ✿ ✓

Iris sibirica varieties

The tough Siberian cousin of the ephemeral bearded iris. Flowering May to June, this large clump forming plant looks wonderful in natural drifts alongside water. Preferring sun or semi shade and a moisture retentive soil, it will also take containerisation but should be re-potted every few years in spring to maintain vigour.

☼ M ✿▲ ✓

Lupinus varieties

Cottage garden stalwarts with flowers ranging from white, through yellow, pink, red and plum. These deciduous plants can be ravaged by molluscs when new leaves emerge in the spring so deal with those early on. Cut off old flowerheads and you may be rewarded with a second smaller flush of blooms later on.

☼◖ S & M ✿ ✓

Paeonia varieties

Long lived, elegant, tough, a great cut flower and good autumn colour are just a few qualities of a Peony. Research is the key to successful planting; decide how much space you have and what colour you would like and then plant and leave well alone save for a feeding, mulching and deadheading.

☼◖ S, M & L ✿▲ ✓✓

Rosa varieties

New disease resistant, repeat blooming roses take far less work than many old-fashioned varieties. For an endless summer display team them with *Clematis* or herbaceous perennials. Stick to the correct pruning regime and ensure you mulch and feed them well to keep the plants strong and blooming for longer.

☼◖ S, M & L ✿ ✓✓

Salvia nemorosa (especially *S. n. 'Caradonna'*)

One of the very best *Salvia* and much loved due to its lengthy flowering period from May through to October. Its strong blue works with paler pastel colours as well as punchy oranges and yellows. This is at its best in full sun in a dry-ish soil. Winter wet can rot it away.

☼◖ S ✿ ✓

Hydrangea aspera

A more unusual *Hydrangea* with hirsute leaves and flat mauve flowers, surrounded by paler bracts in August. A bold plant for a border, it combines well with *Anemone*, *Aster*, evergreen shrubs and ferns. Pruning is not onerous. Given ample water it will grow in a container but natural ground is preferred.

◖● L ✿▲ ✓

Roof terraces and balconies

Daydreaming about garden design is a lovely pastime and thumbing through magazines picking out ideas is a great way to spend a lazy Sunday. Armed with inspiration, it is relatively easy to create a small town or courtyard garden and with a little extra thought you could tackle a basement garden. Roof terraces and balconies, however, are a totally different beast. Over the years I have learned that just because a property is advertised as having a roof terrace, it doesn't mean that the roof can actually be used as a terrace. Many flat roofs are just that: flat and meant to be used as a roof, not as a party zone. Beyond the fact that a flat roof may not be able to support the weight of decking or stone (let alone people and pots), there may be planning restrictions that prevent the use of the roof as a terrace, certainly if by using it as such you have a direct eye-line into a neighbouring property or vice versa. Progressing a design for a roof terrace without undertaking an expert survey would be monumentally stupid. Getting something wrong at ground level is bad, but making a mistake at height could be catastrophic.

The services of a structural engineer are vital. They will be able to tell you the weight-loading capabilities of the terrace or balcony and advise you what you can accommodate comfortably. This is where coordination is required. You may need to supply a scaled drawing (yes, the ever-helpful scaled drawing) with your layout on it and indicative wet weights of planters. Always offer a wet weight as water is heavy and can add many kilograms to the weight of each planter.

Weight is not the only restriction at height. Even just one storey up, the wind is stronger than at ground level. Two storeys up, it is very blustery. The higher you go, the more buffeting the effect of the wind. At height, wind eddies between buildings and constantly changes direction, which means that whatever you plant will need to be anchored down, furniture should be heavy and parasols cannot be used and left up unattended.

If you can counter the weight-loading and buffering of the wind, there is still the problem of access. This is the major design limiter of gardens at height. It may not be possible to use a crane. Even if your budget allows for a crane, there may not be space on the road for one near enough to the roof terrace or balcony. This means that all the materials and plants either have to be transported in a lift or via the stairs by 'landscaper power' alone. It's important to note that lifts are only about 2 metres (6½ foot) high, which radically limits the size of plants and materials (decking boards in particular), and the number of flights of stairs will have an impact on the weight of materials that can be carried up in one go. In addition to the materials that need to be transported upwards, don't forget that the waste needs to come down too!

Given all of these challenges, roof terraces and balconies have a strict list of do's and don'ts. Like basement gardens, think of these as challenges and turn a problem into a fortuitous design feature.

Right: even small rooftops can provide all the elements required from an outside space. There is something magical about a roof terrace where you can see for miles but it is also possible to create privacy and a cosy feel.

Following page: by definition, rooftops are blustery spaces. Working with, rather than against, the elements is sensible. Grasses and trees add movement to otherwise static schemes with heavy elements.

The do's

Roof terraces can seem like daunting spaces to garden but they can revolutionise modern high-rise living and provide a connection with the greater landscape that would otherwise not be there. Greening these spaces is vital for wildlife, so always keep this in mind when thinking about planting your roof, especially if you wish to grow fruit and vegetables.

Do check that you can actually install a roof terrace where you want to. This is the time to ask the experts; architects and planning consultants. An estimate costing of their services is extremely wise prior to any planning or installation works so that you can keep a handle on fees from the outset.

Do employ the services of a structural engineer. Although not an inexpensive process it will mean you know exactly where you stand – hopefully on a very sturdy roof terrace or balcony.

Do contact a crane company. It is a pretty obvious thing to say but crane companies lift larger and heavier things for a living. Their advice, even at the planning stage, will potentially refine your design ideas and process. Ignore their advice at your peril.

Do design carefully. There is no space more challenging to design than a roof terrace. Think long and hard about how you want the space to look once complete, and always consider the ongoing maintenance. What goes up must come down at some point in time.

Do create areas of seclusion. Sitting on a roof terrace can feel like being on a goldfish bowl. Overlooking issues from neighbouring properties at the same height or above could mean you are in full view, so unless you are happy with this then do consider elements to create privacy.

Check that you can actually install a roof terrace where you want to

- This will involve a little bit of digging and perhaps the services of a planning consultant or other experts.

Employ the services of a structural engineer

- If the news is not good and the roof or balcony will not take the weight you wish to install, you have two choices: rectify the structure and increase the load bearing or walk away from the plan if the costs to fix the structure are simply prohibitive.

Contact a crane company

- The least complicated way to move materials onto a roof is by crane. You will need a fully managed and insured lift to do this.
- Ask the crane company to provide a lifting plan and give them as much information as you can for the design so they can work out if one lift or multiple lifts are required. This will determine the length of the permit they apply for as well as the overall cost.

Design carefully

- Keep in mind the implementation of the project when you are planning your design. More than any other type of garden, the practical aspects of creating a roof terrace or balcony are intimately intertwined with considerations of what the garden will look like. Built-in structures and furniture stand less chance of being swept away by high winds, so consider these rather than free-standing pieces – do check what is permitted first though.
- Make sure there is access to water for irrigation on the roof.
- Ensure the drainage is adequate before you start.

Create areas of seclusion

- Try to create areas of shelter and privacy by using small trees in large planters.
- If permissions allow and the structure can take it, a small pergola can be an effective way to create some shade and privacy. Compared to a tree, a pergola may provide a more sympathetic architectural link to the building.
- If the building structure permits, an automated awning with a wind sensor that allows the awning to be fully retracted, even when you are not around, offers shade by day and heat by night without shading the interior rooms of the property as tree canopies and a pergola would do.

Choose appropriate hard-landscaping materials

- Wind, driving rain and fierce sun all have an impact on the longevity of hard-landscaping materials. Decking will fade in strong sun, stone will become dirty and green when exposed to water and sunlight (although this is really the same in any garden space) and any reflective material could end up creating a blinding effect or, worse, reflect and refract the sunlight onto other surfaces, causing burns and scorch marks.
- Many terraces at height require the installation of hard landscaping on a pedestal system to allow for drainage to the roof underneath. Make sure there is adequate space to allow for pedestals through the design process and speak to your structural engineer to ensure that point-loaded pressure on the pedestals has no implications on the roof surface. This is most common over a waterproof membrane as any pressure on this may invalidate its warranty.

Select plants that will cope with the site and situation

- Most roof terraces and balconies catch the sun, so planting with this in mind means a palette of plants that thrive in Mediterranean climates or coastal areas, where the effects of sun and wind can be dramatic. Plants that like the sun often prefer to be dry at the root. Less irrigation on a roof means less to go wrong!
- Inform your structural engineer if a plant that is only small when newly planted is likely to grow and bulk out quickly as its assumed final weight will need to be calculated into the scheme.

The don'ts

Roofs – they are not the place to experiment if you are a roof virgin. Previously in this book I have suggested do's and don'ts for different types of small gardens. Roofs are the spaces where often the don'ts outweigh the do's. If you are in any doubt, enlist the services of a garden designer, landscape architect and/or structural engineer.

Don't assume that a flat roof can be turned into a terrace. Just because a flat roof surface is available it does not necessarily mean that from it you will be able to create a usble terrace. There are a multitude of reasons why you may not be able to. These include weight restrictions, planning restrictions, access issues and cost – everything at height carries a premium as it may need to be double, triple or even quadruple handled before it gets to its final position.

Don't select lightweight furniture. Roof terraces and balconies need heavyweight furniture to prevent it blowing around or – even worse – flying off the terrace. If you are going to use waterproof covers to protect your furniture, make sure these are secured very tightly to prevent them acting like sails and working themselves free.

Don't leave items such as pots and sculptural elements unsecured. Anything that has its head above the parapet is likely to be blasted by the wind. Anchor absolutely everything that you can, batten down the hatches, stay the mainsail ...! If you use planters, ensure they are bottom heavy; tall and tapered planters may look elegant but they won't stay upright for long. Instead, opt for squat containers with a wide base which can be anchored for stability.

Don't use a normal planting medium. A normal loam-based soil is heavy, especially when wet. Speak to a trusted soil supplier and ask for a roof-terrace mix. This usually contains a small percentage of loam with compost and an added lightweight substrate as well as a slow-release fertiliser. A palette of drought-tolerant plants will be quite happy in this mix, which should always have a free-draining layer underneath it.

Don't overdo the lighting. There is a very fine line between enough light and too much light. Consider neighbours as well as wildlife when implementing any lighting. Uplights on a roof are not really going to be very much use unless you have installed trees, so ensure that the light is focused down into the space to create an intimate and welcoming effect rather than a big and bold statement. Neighbouring properties will value your discretion here.

Don't be vague. Ensure all elements of the design are sampled, agreed and signed off long before installation. If an item of furniture or a plant or a container has to be lifted onto a roof terrace or balcony using a crane, you may need a crane to get it back down again if you subsequently decide it isn't warranted in the scheme. Ensure you are 100% sure that you will like the items before they are put into place.

Don't remove balustrading to the perimeter of the terrace. Balustrading is installed for a very good reason. It might well block your eye-line when you are sitting down but it will prevent you from falling over the edge. This is another one of those it-is-not-rocket-science principles.

Don't plant anything that likes to be shaded and cool. Most plants that like to be hot and dry can also cope with a degree of neglect, making a roof terrace a slightly less maintenance-heavy garden than a basement courtyard. (This is mainly because any debris in the form of fallen leaves is blown away the wind.) Avoid planting excessively messy plants such as bamboo. If any plant is guaranteed to shrivel to a desiccated mess within days on a roof terrace, it is bamboo. Ornamental grasses look wonderful billowing in the breeze on a roof terrace, but do make sure they have adequate water otherwise they too will frazzle very quickly.

Plants for sunny rooftops and balconies

Roof terraces and balconies work well with plants that do not or cannot move a great deal when buffeted by the wind. A planting scheme would look pretty awful if it was motionless – so some movement is essential – just select your plants with care and find a happy harmonious balance between static and ethereal plants. There are lots of bulbs that like to be hot and dry. These are a quick gain when added to planting on a roof. *Allium*, *Acidonathera*, *Trithia*, *Gladiolus communis*, *Crocus*, *Iris*, *Euconis* and *Crocosmia* all add colour at little expense. You may need to replace these every few years to keep the display looking bright but this is easily and simply achieved in the autumn.

Wouldn't it be wonderful if our cityscape was clothed in greenery? Layering up small spaces from basements to rooftops diminishes the effect of even the hardest of hard landscaping.

Aeonium varieties

Fleshy leaves are arranged in circular ever decreasing rosettes on chunky stems. Plant where there is shelter from wind and appreciate the dense colours of the green or near black foliage. A plant that adds drama but in cold, wet or really windy areas winter protection, even when frost free, may be required. Excellent drainage is a must.

☼ S ✿☘ ✓

Agave americana

Sometimes called *Yucca americana*. These plants have unfriendly serrated barbs along the leaves. A very 'look but don't touch' kind of plant. Glaucous blue or striped green and yellow are the commonest forms and due to their prickly nature do look best as feature plants with a simple grit mulch underneath which also aids drainage the root.

☼ M ☘ ✓

Butia capitata

A fine leaved palm tree that looks like it would be completely shredded to pieces by the wind. In fact, it always seems to come off better than *Chamerops* and *Trachycarpus* so it would be my pick out of the three for a roof terrace. These are plants of stature though and will warrant a conversation with your structural engineer.

☼ M&L ☘ ✓✓

Echium webbii

An hairy sub-shrub perfect for a hot roof where it should, unless the winter is devastating, survive year to year. Blue candles appear in early summer and should be removed afterwards. *Echium* can cause stomach upsets if ingested and its leaves may irritate bare skin. Plant with later flowering plants to extend seasonal interest. *Gaura* and *Penstemmon* would work well.

☼ M ✿ ✓

Eriobotrya varieties

Loquats, from large slightly hairy pleated leaves and plentiful fruits to small smooth leaves and the prettiest of pale pink flowers. These are plants that like to be warm though. Give them some shelter and ensure they are watered and they will grow and fill out steadily. Under-planting can be simple – a swathe of grasses or low growing *Sedum*.

☼ M&L ✿ ✓✓

Festuca glauca

A neat hummock forming grass in a strong glaucous blue with panicles of toasty brown flowers in late summer. Often not a long-lived plant but given a very free draining site and good light it will reward for several years with only a quick comb through in the spring on your part. Not one for hayfever sufferers allergic to grasses.

☼ S ✿☘ ✓

Gaura lindheimeri

Wiry stems that bely their fragile appearance are in fact surprisingly indestructible. Topped with masses of white or pink flowers, this is a good plant to weave through others (*Agapanthus* for one) for a naturalistic effect. As an added bonus its leaves change with the seasons to warm red tones, so do not cut them down until the spring.

☼ S ✿ ✓

Griselinia littoralis

This an extremely useful plant. An evergreen that can be lightly clipped but that will take full sun and wind. It is a plant that will cope with coastal exposure too so its credentials for hot and dry are covered. Shiny apple green rounded leaves are a great backdrop to small *Escallonia* varieties or more tropical *Echium*.

☼ M&L ☘ ✓

Lavandula varieties

Scented, sturdy and a lover of hot weather. Plant high and dry on a roof and you will be rewarded by a dense mass of purple blooms humming with bees. To keep your plants compact remove faded flowers after blooming and trim again in April, do not though cut into old wood though – the plant will not regenerate.

☼ S&M ✿ ✓

Olea europaea

The olive tree, reliable, long-lived, evergreen, copes with pollution, drought, wind and extreme sun. There possibly isn't anything quite as perfect to plant on a roof as an Olive. If you would like an old characterful gnarly one, then speak to your structural engineer and a crane company as they can weigh upwards of a ton and sometimes more.

☼ M & L 🐦 ✓

Penstemon **varieties**

Semi-evergreen perennials that will thrive on a sunny roof or balcony. Tubular flowers are produced in the summer for months on end and it is not unheard of for them to carry on flowering right up until Christmas if conditions allow. White, pink, coral and the darkest of purples make this a stalwart choice for any sunny planting scheme.

☼◖ S ✿ ✓

Pinus mugo 'Mops'

Many pines will grow on roofs, this just happens to be small, compact and well-behaved. Conifers, out of fashion for so long are making their way to the front again, often with multiple stems and interesting shapes, this smaller variety offers great punctuation to softer planting as well as complimenting shrubs such as *Cistus*, *Rosmarinus* and *Pittosporum*.

☼ S, M & L 🐦 ✓

Pittosporum tobira **varieties**

Like *Griselinia* these plants are coastal friendly plants, love the sun and in this case have the added bonus of wonderful sweet-scented flowers that top out the light green or variegated foliage in the summer. So versatile that they can also take being clipped into shape, if topiary is your thing. Pair with *Olea*, *Oleander* and *Eriobotrya* for bulk.

☼◖ S, M & L ✿🐦 ✓✓

Sempervivum **varieties**

These lovely plants are beyond low maintenance. Plant them, walk away and they will just get on with it in the main by themselves. Your only task is to ensure when planting that they have a very gritty soil and are not shaded out by other planting, that and maybe a vine weevil check every so often.

☼◖ S ✿🐦 ✓

Stipa tenuissima

An elegant, free moving grass. Like Festuca it too is not long lived but its movement brings lower storey planting schemes to life. Planted to catch the last of the evening sun it shines in golden tones and works well under-planted with *Allium* – their spent flowerheads increasing the halo effect. Add sun loving herbaceous perennials or herbs as companions.

◖● S 🐦 ✓

Yucca gloriosa

Spiky doesn't really do this plant justice. The ends of the leaves are like hypodermic syringes. Always plant them so they are not in eye-line when standing or sitting or anywhere they can be accidently backed into. For all of their static nature they command a presence and absolutely warrant their place. Very free draining soil is a must.

☼◖ M ✿🐦 ✓

Yucca rostrata

A soft and touchy-feely *Yucca*, well almost. Purchased at size these plants are very old (command a price tag) and should be planted with reverence. Their black stems and top knot of blue grey leaves make a striking combination which can be softened with an under-planting of *Sedum* and *Salvia* if you wish or simply mulched with a decorative gravel.

☼ M 🐦 ✓✓

Woody herbs

Thyme, Oregano, Rosemary, Bay and Sage (pictured). If you want to grow herbs for culinary use, then the hot dry conditions of a roof terrace or balcony are ideal. Give them space, a gritty free draining soil and don't plant anything too close to shade them out and you will have a plentiful and fresh supply of herbs all year round.

☼ S & M ✿🐦 ✓

How to deal with existing structures and plants

The pros and cons of gardening in small spaces

There is a lot to be said for gardening in small spaces. Not only are small gardens relatively affordable in terms of the design budget, but also their bijou-nature means that their upkeep won't cost you an arm or a leg, nor will they take up too much of your valuable downtime to maintain. The downside to such green spaces is that they are often overlooked from many angles and share neighbours' walls or fences, which could be unattractive, dominating or downright unstable.

As with any design, it is always easiest to start with a blank canvas, but that is unlikely to be the case with a town garden so you will need to be creative about your boundaries and views. If your garden is enclosed by fences or trellis, you will probably discover that not all of it belongs to you. If your garden is bounded by a mishmash of fencing and/or walls, is it necessary to unify your boundaries? Well, in an ideal world the answer is yes. Unifying the boundaries of small spaces really does help to bring a scheme together. It reduces the number of things that can distract the eye on the boundaries, ensures that the scheme will be calmer and allows you to create and control elements of interest where you actually want them. You may find the use of the word 'control' an odd terminology, but all design contains an element of control to enable you to create the picture on the ground that is in your mind. The ability to draw the viewer's eye to the areas you want and build drama is what makes a good design great.

The following pages explore some common obstacles that you may come across in town gardens, along with some potential quick (and not so quick) fixes to make them work with your scheme. This is not, by any stretch of the imagination, a comprehensive list, just a selection of the problems I encounter regularly.

Previous page: the elephant in the room here is the grill concealing an air conditioning unit. When treated tonally the same as other elements in the garden its impact is reduced. When lit, the fire and flames draw the eye even though their presence is much smaller than the louvered box that hangs above.

Right: stripes and checks; we know how to wear clothes to best flatter us. In principle, the same rules can be applied to our gardens. Vertical lines lengthen and squares anchor the scheme. Dark tones also work in the same way to reduce the impact of large elements.

Boundary fences and walls

Shared fences or walls can be a contentious issue between neighbours.

Any work to replace or renovate these boundaries should be undertaken only after discussions with your neighbour. Discussing your intentions with your neighbour won't necessarily prevent any animosity over the subject but it will at least forewarn them that you would like to alter a boundary detail. These conversations are vital if your neighbour has climbing plants trained to their boundary. Fences and walls should always be replaced over the shared boundary line and when both parties agree.

Is there a height limit for the boundaries?

It is advisable to check with your local authority whether there is a maximum height permitted for your garden boundaries. Height restrictions may vary from authority to authority. Keep in mind that the trellis on top of a fence is often included in the overall height.

Does the wall or fence belong to you?

You would be surprised at how many oddities there could be in property boundaries where fence lines may have moved over time, and often the deeds to a person's property have revealed that what they expected to belong to them actually didn't. The deeds to your home may influence the decisions you make about your boundaries and whether you wish to foot the bill for the works or see if your neighbours would contribute towards the cost of the boundary in question if it is theirs. In order to minimise any disruption to your neighbour, sometimes it is simplest to concede the hundred or so millimetres (4 inches) it takes to install a new fence or trellis on your own property rather than on the shared boundary line.

What type of fence or trellis should you choose?

Depending on the materials you choose, your fence and trellis can either be a feature of the garden (usually best in minimal schemes) or visually disappear into the background. Boundary treatments are often a large proportion of the budget as their visual appeal is important, particularly for minimal schemes that require careful detailing. For softer schemes, you can afford to install less-expensive fences and trellis as they are most likely to be covered in planting for much of the year.

What do I need to consider if there are low walls between the gardens?

Are the walls sound? Many old brick walls do not have foundations and so can be 'live', which is a great way of describing something that is wobbly and likely to fall over if it is topped with trellis and heavily planted with climbers. Ask a landscaper or structural engineer to assess the walls before doing anything. It is better to spend money on an assessment first as the costs to rebuild a wall are considerable.

What about high walls from surrounding buildings?

High walls from neighbouring properties are often commonplace in urban gardens. They can shade and dominate a scheme and sometimes there is simply nothing that you can do to screen them completely. If you have the room, it is worth considering using tall plants that will offer some buffering to the wall but won't hide it completely – bamboo and silver birch would both work well. If your budget allows, you could deploy a vertical green wall, although it will need to be fixed to the wall so you should seek the building owner's permission – tricky if it is an apartment block and each property is freehold.

Built structures

Over the years I have encountered a variety of unexpected structures in gardens, from the odd to the frankly ridiculous.

- **Air-raid shelters with asbestos roofs:** These relics from World War II are thankfully becoming fewer and farther between. It is possible to deal with the structure of the shelter, though it will not be easy (they were meant to survive bomb blasts, after all), but the asbestos roof will require specialist removal due to its poisonous nature and the fact that you cannot put it into a normal skip or take it to a waste dump.

- **Over-engineered walls:** I have encountered many walls that looked as if they would disintegrate just by looking at them, only to discover that they had been reinforced with canteens of cutlery, garden tools and even bed frames. Generally, walls that have been built by a not-so-competent DIYer go one of two ways: either they give way with ease or are so over-engineered that they take three times the amount of time to remove than you would have thought.

- **Inconvenient pathways:** Here, I'm thinking of the ubiquitous 1930s pathway that runs either to each side of a garden or straight down the middle. There will never be just one path. They will be at least two layers deep, or even three if you are unlucky.

- **Unusual mounds:** Always double-check any feature that looks like it might be hiding something else. You would be amazed at how many tree stumps or low walls get 'accidentally' covered over with soil to create features rather than being removed from the site. Unfortunately, 'surprises' like this will now become your problem to deal with.

- **Air-conditioning units:** Items like this are not easily masked by planting. The air that they pump out is desiccating and can be devastating to plants up to 3 metres (10 foot) away. Air-conditioning units should always be plotted at the survey stage because, if they are to remain, they will influence your design layout. Screening with timber or acoustic louvres is a harder solution than concealing with planting, but it will require less ongoing maintenance.

- **Boiler vents:** Scalding clouds of billowing steam, now that is something that plants absolutely will not like. What you may not realise is that when steam condenses in the same place on a wall for any length of time it will mark that wall, and in areas of hard water an unsightly limescale crust will form that will collect pollution rapidly and turn brown and black. There is little that can be done here, though you may be able to box the vents, providing you receive the OK from a gas-safe engineer, as there may be a requirement of free air space around the vent. On the plus side, these vents do warm the air in cold courtyard spaces and you may be surprised how quickly any planting grows. Just do not plant anything too near the vent.

- **Fibreglass replicas of Mr Blobby's house (if you remember 1990s, Saturday-night television, you will know what this is):** I don't think there is any answer to this type of problem, other than its complete removal, pronto!

I have learned to expect the unexpected and to poke my nose into shrubberies to make sure I evaluate everything at the outset to avoid complications later on. If it looks odd and grabs your attention, then the likelihood is it warrants a second glance and a good prod with a garden fork.

'I have learned to expect the unexpected and to poke my nose into shrubberies to make sure I evaluate everything at the outset to avoid complications.'

Drainage

There is no point in creating a new garden if the drainage does not work on the land that you have. Drainage issues are even more complicated in small spaces, which often are landlocked, below ground level or elevated at the top of a building. If a garden is wet despite very little rainfall around the time that you survey the property, there may be something wrong below ground. The answer may be as simple as an old soakaway that has failed or it could be that what appears to be a drain gulley is actually not connected to anything at all. Inadequate drainage can be a common problem in basement spaces and if the garden is on a clay soil, which is slow to drain (if not borderline impermeable), then the problem can be exacerbated.

When the drainage fails on roof terraces, the problem generally doesn't present itself outside of the property. Unfortunately, it often shows up only too late when it finds its way through a roof membrane and into the room below. If you inherit a new roof, providing a structural engineer gives you the OK, you shouldn't need to waterproof it. However, an old roof is always worth re-waterproofing before you tackle an installation. With guarantees of twenty years or more for re-waterproofing work, you can rest happy knowing that even if a drain does somehow become blocked the water will not enter the building. To aid water dispersion on a roof, the majority of paving or decking needs to be constructed on pedestals to allow a free-draining area under the walked-on surface that will discharge water rapidly. Ensuring this space stays free of debris is essential: you should install liftable access panels within the hard surfaces so the roof can be checked once or twice a year.

Existing planting

Not all existing planting needs to be removed in order to create a new garden, especially if you are on a budget. Admittedly, you may inherit a scheme that contains nothing but tarmac and shopping trolleys, but when you undertake your survey you should always evaluate the planting and consider whether any of it has enough merit to remain. Whether a plant has merit can be assessed in several ways, but in essence you should ask yourself:

- How much life does the plant have left in it? Is it worth retaining?
- Does it come under the protection of a Conservation Area or have a Tree Preservation Order? (see page 52)
- If it has outgrown its space, is it possible to renovate or move it?
- Is it in the way? Can it be moved?
- Will it fit stylistically with your new ideas?
- Is it worth lifting, dividing and potting on to create more of the same plant, which can then be grown on ready to plant out in the new scheme?

If the consensus is that the existing planting needs to be removed and the plants would continue to grow and thrive after being lifted, there are many horticultural charities and guerrilla gardeners who would love to take the unwanted plants off your hands, so putting them into a skip should be the very last resort.

Although it would be absolutely wonderful if summer lasted all year and every plant had the decency to retain its leaves at the precise time of year when you want to identify it, the reality is that you may need to be able to identify plants that are bare of leaves or have yet to emerge from the ground. If your skills are lacking in the plant-identification department, you could be missing out on some rarities that are worth their place in your new scheme. It's wise to invest in a good illustrated plant encyclopedia or to use online plant identification apps. You may need to identify plants from their bark or bud structure alone, which will require research and care.

Sometimes you may wish to keep an existing plant in order to preserve the essence of a space. It probably sounds a bit hokey but I believe that gardens have a special feeling if the previous owners have treasured the plants, and reducing the original planting to ground level to create something shiny and brand new never sits right with me. If you can retain something of the past, the future space you create will be all the better for it. Having said that, a lot of small urban gardens you inherit are unloved concrete spaces and there is nothing you can do to them that won't improve them. The task is simple: add greenery and all will be well.

Existing elements or plantings can add maturity to a scheme. You may find that under a canopy an existing plant has an interesting stem (or stems) and that you can clear some of the foliage to expose its form.

Design solutions for tricky spaces

Boundary screening to suit all budgets

Fencing

Ready-made wooden fence panels are inexpensive, readily available and easy to install. It is important to check you have adequate access if you need to take the panels through a property. With dimensions of about 1800 x 1800 x 50mm (70 x 70 x 2in), the panels will be narrow enough to fit through doorways, but they won't go around a 90-degree corner. Wood, Willow and split bamboo also make effective and inexpensive fences. This cost does reflect the lifespan which is not long – ten years at most.

Bespoke fencing can be specially made for your garden and should be installed by a landscaper. This option will allow you to customise and coordinate your fence and trellis to your design. Wood is often the best choice but metal also works well and is most appropriate in schemes where you want the boundary to be part of the design rather than covered by plants.

Previous page: bold and strong are the key design rules for small gardens. Add height where possible and be bold in colour and form.

Right: if your desire is for a garden dressed all year round, then a palette of evergreens is the one for you. You can always add punchy colour with furniture or keep it muted and elegant.

Pleached trees

Pleached hedges look a bit like they are on stilts. Evergreen varieties are available, but the most successful tree varieties to pleach are *Carpinus* (hornbeam) and *Fagus* (beech). Both create dense panels of light-green leaves in the spring and summer, turning golden in the autumn. Most plants will hold their dead leaves on the branches through the winter before the new leaves emerge in the spring. Pleached trees enforce a gentle formality to a design and work well both with other topiary forms and plantings with a softer perennial palette.

Unless you have twelve-foot ceilings, wide doorways and no objection to an upwards of 250kg (550lb) tree being manhandled through your house (and realistically, why would you want this?), a side entrance or the ability to mechanically lift the tree into your garden are the best options. Pleached trees require clipping once a year – you may wish to ask a professional to do this for you if ladderwork is not your forte. As with most things in life, the larger and more mature the tree, the more instantly attractive it is and consequently the costlier.

———

'Pleached trees enforce a gentle formality to a design and work well both with other topiary forms and plantings with a softer perennial palette.'

———

Climbing plants

- Once settled in, large-growing, self-clinging *Parthenocissus tricuspidata* and *Hedera* varieties (ivy) will soon clothe walls and boundaries. *Parthenocissus tricuspidata* is not evergreen but it does turn fiery red in the autumn before dropping its leaves and is worth its place for that alone. Any self-clinging plant has tenacious feet, so keep foliage trimmed back of any loose masonry, painted window frames or even glass as when the foliage is cleared, an imprint of the feet can remain. This will detract from the building façade.
- *Hydrangea seemannii* is a well-behaved, evergreen climbing plant. It takes a while to establish but it is ideal for small walls and fences. You could also try the equally lovely, equally slow-growing *Pileostegia viburnoides*.
- If you don't already know about evergreen *Clematis*, *C. armandii* may be a bit of a revelation to you. It has very un-*Clematis*-like oval, dark-green, leathery leaves and in the late winter and early spring it is covered by masses (and I mean *masses*) of white or pale-pink flowers that smell wonderful. It will want

to scale heights very quickly, so persist in pulling it laterally if you can to keep it within your space.
- *Wisteria* varieties will definitely clothe your boundaries – and potentially your neighbour's, too. In order to keep your *Wisteria* in check, it will require radical pruning twice a year in January and July, which will result in the plant producing the most wonderful scented display with hanging racemes of lilac-blue or white flowers in late spring to early summer. Don't leave it to its own devices, though, as it will very happily put on twenty feet in a year. Be warned: in the autumn it can fill your gutters and drains with deep piles of leaves that somehow manage to bond themselves together in ways that block the flow of water very effectively!

Trees and large shrubs

- *Betula* varieties (birch) work really well in town gardens. Birches are not dense, they do not grow to be massive and their white or coloured bark goes a long way to highlight a winter scheme. Birches work well with all manner of other plants: a simple combination would be *Hydrangea* 'Annabelle', *Hosta* 'Patriot', *Polystichum polyblepharum* and *Digitalis* 'Pam's Choice'. Other larger plants for small gardens are often best as multi-stem forms as they add character; *Amelanchier canadensis*, *Parrotia persica* and many of the *Magnolia* family all contribute to the overall effect of small garden spaces.
- Evergreen *Phyllostachys viridis* and *P. nigra* (green- and black-stemmed bamboos) are tall and elegant, though they can be messy when they drop their leaves. Plant them with care because, despite being commonly described as 'clump formers', once established they are liable to spread. Protecting the boundaries between yourself and your neighbour will be essential, otherwise the bamboo's shoots will run under walls and fences and push up on the other side wherever they can. These plants work well with other leafy forms that appreciate some shade, including *Dicksonia antarctica*, *Hosta*, *Rodgersia aesculifolia*, herbaceous ferns, small evergreen shrubs, *Pachysandra*, *Helleborus* and *Tiarella*.
- *Cupressus sempervirens* (pencil conifer) can be positioned in a regular rhythm that will not form a solid boundary, rather it will create a sense of a boundary with glimpses through. Full sun is required and perhaps a bright white wall to the rear to reflect light at the back of the plant, where it would otherwise slowly become bare. Be warned, though, the less mature the plant, the more likely it is to bend and grow out of shape, so this may be a plant that warrants a mature purchase. Hot and dry are the elements that *Cupressus* live for, so there is no point in grouping them with plants that like to be cool and wet at the root. Woody herbs, *Pittosporum*, *Hebe*, *Agave* and ornamental grasses would all make very good bedfellows.

Big plants in little spaces? Always! Large architectural forms, but less of them, will make a space appear more generous.

Masking views

Choosing the right structure for you

Using structures such as pergolas or garden buildings to mask views can be tricky. However, with some care and thought you can not only mask a view but also create a focal point within your design scheme. Below are some structures and their placement to consider for your new scheme.

Pergolas

A pergola in the garden is a lovely feature. Not only does it afford privacy from prying eyes above but it also creates shelter and shade and can be planted with an array of scented climbing plants. In minimal schemes, pergolas can be left unplanted and will add an architectural element to your garden.

Sheds and summerhouses

Creating storage areas that are attractive and usable is really important in a small space. If you can hide away cushions and bikes, old paint tins and plant pots, your small garden will always be the nicer for it. Siting a shed or summerhouse can be more difficult than the placement of a lightweight pergola. They are bulky structures and will protrude above adjacent fences or walls, even if your aim is to mask a view with them, so a conversation with your neighbour might be worthwhile here, as well as potentially your local authority to find out their rules for garden structures. If your neighbour has a shed or summerhouse then siting yours at the same point on your side of the boundary will mask theirs – sometimes the simplest solutions work the best.

Awnings and shade sails

Garden awnings and shade sails are useful in small spaces because they are not necessarily permanent and can be deployed only when you need them. They are usually made from high-tensile materials that are washable, which is essential when they are positioned under trees as pollen and debris can stain. These structures can look really magical at night with candle lanterns lighting them and they always feel more impromptu and intimate than the more solid and dependable pergola. Think of them as allowing you to go camping in your garden – just throw some rugs and cushions on the floor and relax!

Vertical green walls

Much beloved by architects for their ability to green buildings, vertical green walls are tricky to site and install. Yes, they could clothe a 30 metre (98 foot) high building with greenery but unless your pockets are very deep indeed that may well be financially prohibitive. In small gardens the wall onto which you intend to attach a green wall may not belong to you. Consequently, you may need to use the services of a structural engineer to create a stand-alone structure to support the system. If you are able to install a green wall then do so, but be prepared for the ongoing and costly maintenance bills associated with it. If not, the dependable *Trachelospermum jasminoides* grown up tensioned wires is a very good viable alternative indeed.

You may want to block a view or just blur the edges. Chose a screen accordingly, considering how much you wish to hide or absorb a view. Remember that a solid screen will most likely add shade too.

Turning a problem into a feature

Sometimes it isn't possible to mask a view or an unattractive building or large wall. There are times when adding elements to a design will only make it busy or complicated or, in the case of small gardens, take up too much of the footprint of the garden to warrant their inclusion. When this is the case you need to rethink the idea of screening and instead turn the eyesore into a feature. You can do this in several ways:

- Create a focal point within the garden that draws the eye away from the offending view. This could be a water feature, a sculpture, an architectural plant or even a large decorative urn or planter. It doesn't have to be big and expensive, it just needs to catch your eye and your interest.
- Paint the unsightly article a bright colour, add an artwork or even graffiti and make it take centre stage. This is a bold choice, though, so be sure before you do it!
- Create angles and different spaces within the garden that break up the eye-line so the offending feature cannot be seen directly from the property. Laser-cut filigree screens, pleached trees (see page 104) and – if space and light levels allow – ornamental grasses will all add height and softly moving interest that is distracting in a good way.

Turning a problem into a feature is a much bolder choice than trying to mask an eyesore, but done cleverly it can create a unique effect.

Screening issues for roof terraces

Views are to be celebrated on a roof terrace. It is from here that a cityscape can best be appreciated, especially at night. However, there are some rooftop items you might want to consider screening.

Practical objects such as vents, air-conditioning units, service shafts and window-cleaning equipment may all be found on a roof, though perhaps they matter less in this context than at ground level as this is exactly where you would expect to find them. If you can accommodate their screening within a design without masking a view you'd like to preserve, do so but you may find that the view takes precedence and these functional elements can be 'overlooked' in favour of the rooftops and horizon. Be warned: a newly constructed building may have specific rules and covenants that prevent you from screening such items or you may have permission to screen them but need to apply the vernacular architecture of the building to your design scheme and submit it for approval before any works can commence.

Any vertical boundary on a roof that catches the wind and could act as a sail should be checked and approved by a structural engineer who can advise how to secure and fix these elements safely. An engineer will also be able to work out how much of these structures should be permeable in order to allow wind to blow through them rather than buffet against them.

> ## 'The truer you are to your original vision, the more the garden will be an extension of you.'

A thorough evaluation is essential

I wish I could shout the following from every rooftop – and basement and courtyard – but I fear I would get some funny looks at the very least. So I'll shout it here instead:

Carefully and thoroughly evaluating your site before you embark upon a design and plan is not only a good idea, it is essential to the design process from the outset. Lift drain covers; poke shrubbery; wiggle walls; measure access; identify trees and other plants; make notes on the good, the bad and the ugly; take photos and examine them carefully – you will be amazed at the things you discover in a photo that you somehow missed in reality.

The more accurate your scaled plan, the less you will need to change on the ground and the truer you will be to your original vision. The truer you are to your original vision, the more the garden will be an extension of you and the way you wish to live and garden.

Plan, plan, plan – the finished effect will be far the better for it.

Linear, vertical elements, changes in level, textural walling; this should be visually jarring, but because each space and material has been thoroughly considered it is not. Pops of colour add interest and a muted planting scheme makes it very easy on the eye.

Selecting materials

Hard-landscaping materials

I have touched on this a little in the preceding chapters but since hard-landscaping materials really do form the backbone of your garden – and are likely to be the costliest element – the thought process behind which materials to select and why is one worth expanding upon.

It should be stated in no uncertain terms that no hard-landscaping material used in a town or city will remain pristine. Pollution from cars and aeroplanes, general litter and natural elements like sun, water and leaf and pollen drop will all combine to etch and disfigure the surfaces of stone, decking, render and bricks. Is there anything that can be done to prevent this? The short and somewhat unpalatable answer is no. The solutions to these problems are ongoing regular maintenance and a sensible and practical choice of materials that will suit the way you wish to live (for example, the amount of time you wish to dedicate to your broom), the look you wish to achieve and the budget you have set yourself. Below are the major factors to consider when selecting materials.

What is the look you wish to achieve?
- Light or dark?
- Smooth or textured?
- Traditional or contemporary? Minimal or maximal?

What is your budget?
- Is your budget high, low or somewhere comfortably in the middle? The cost will hinge on the amount of material you require. It is always worth spending as much as you can on hard-landscaping materials for a small space because they will be seen year-round and all in one go.

How much time do you have for maintenance?
- It would be very hard to design a garden that requires absolutely no maintenance. Even the term 'low maintenance' can be a misnomer. The best you can do is select the materials that suit your way of life. Ask yourself the following questions: Do you want to maintain the garden yourself? If so, how much time can you dedicate to it? If not, can you afford to pay someone else to maintain it for you?

What are the access points to your garden?
- Can you safely and with ease transport the materials you wish to use from the point of delivery through to their intended locations? Access through a property, along a narrow side entrance or up onto a roof all pose their own specific problems.
- Complicated access with oversized or impractical materials could easily push the cost of your project skywards. Or may result in materials not being able to be used and needing to be returned to the supplier, if at all possible, after you have taken delivery of them.
- Always triple-check the specifications for bespoke items before you place an order because they absolutely cannot be returned.

From sandstone to limestone, granite to slate, as well as the more unusual porphyry, gneiss and schist, the numerous types of stone to choose from can be boggling.

Previous page: Bold but undeniably brilliant. A smooth wall contrasts natural stacked stone and appropriate planting, demonstrating how hard and soft landscaping can wonderfully go hand in hand.

Paving

Although absolutely not an all-encompassing list, the varieties I discuss below cover a broad spectrum of options, including notes on their potential uses and upkeep.

Laying paving

It is worth noting here that there are many ways to lay stone:

- You can lay paving on a full bed of wet sand and cement over a machine-compacted MOT Type 1 sub-base. Occasionally white cement is used to prevent any grey colour from normal cement pulling through the stone.
- Paving can be affixed using exterior adhesive over a concrete screed.
- You can install pedestals to support the paving. Here you will need to ensure your stone is thicker than normal and some stones, such as Yorkstone, if laid in large formats could require cutting at 50–70mm (2–3in) thick, which will add a huge amount to cost and may have an implication on the sub-structure they are laid over, especially on a roof.

The predominance of stone surfaces in our towns and cities means that drainage is a big issue. Laying paving on pedestals will help improve drainage. Another option is full-draining wet bed. If a basement garden is already below the water table it should go without saying that this option will not work here, instead you will need to send your drainage off site.

A little note about grouting

If you thought that selecting your paving slabs was challenging, deciding how to grout them may push you over the edge. So where do you start? Below is a very simple set of guidelines:

- Grouting for traditional paving: Use a sand-and-cement grout with 8–10mm (0.31–0.39in) wide recessed joints between slabs to allow water to disperse.
- Grouting for contemporary paving: Use exterior tile grout with 3–5mm (0.12–0.2in) joints between slabs. This type of grout comes in a multitude of shades so try to pick one a fraction darker than the slab.
- Grouting for permeable paving: Brush kiln-dried sand between butt-jointed slabs or setts. This is a quick and not very costly method but the ongoing maintenance will be greater than for solid-jointed slabs as weeds can and will seed into the crevices. At certain times of the year, keeping on top of germinating seedlings can be a time-consuming task.

If you are in any doubt, your stone supplier should be able to help you make an informed decision.

Clay pavers make an eye-catching floor that seems to transcend fashion, being both traditional and contemporary. Style with either bold heavy furniture or lightweight designer pieces, add some soft planting, *et voila*, a garden that will stand the test of time.

Sandstone

A commonly used stone with good slip resistance at a good price, sandstone is available in a wide range of colours from creams to greys. Generally, it is a variable stone, often with banding and fossils, which are part of its charm. If you are looking for a stone without any variation, this is not the stone for you – unless you order a significant amount extra and sort through the delivery to pick out only the stones that you want. Sandstone can be supplied riven (akin to the surface of old Yorkstone) or sawn, which is more appropriate for contemporary schemes. It is incredibly versatile and can be cut into large-format regular slabs or small setts, as well as more organic shapes. Yorkstone is a sandstone and can be supplied reclaimed or newly sawn. It is different to the sandstones most suppliers sell which are from India. Yorkstone colours range from buff to grey with iron banding whilst Indian sandstones can be green, grey, pink and buff.

Limestone

Limestone is widely used but tends to be more expensive than sandstone. It comes in a range of colours from black through to cream and can be riven or smooth finished. Limestone is more slippery than sandstone, which means that it should be laid with more caution around areas that will be reliably wet. It often requires specific laying techniques so it is always worth consulting with your supplier regarding the best laying method.

Granite

A totally bombproof stone, granite is hard-wearing and as tough as nails. It warrants a contemporary design scheme where it can shine in its own right. However, granite is not to everyone's taste, often conjuring thoughts of cemeteries. This very flexible stone not only works easily as paving and cladding but also can be sculpted or cut into shapes to create feature elements. Granite has one of the widest colourways in the stone world: all are rather speckled and sparkly in shades from grey and silver to pink, green and black. It can be sawn, hammered or flamed. Granite will not support a gently riven surface as its composition does not work that way.

Slate

There is a very good reason why slate is used as a roofing material: it is impervious to water. However, this quality means that it can be very treacherous when used as a paving material, so you will need to be very careful of its slip factor. Slate works well in and around water features and as a decorative aggregate. Due to its layered nature slate can delaminate or flake away, therefore avoid using it anywhere where it could get knocked and bumped. Often one of trickiest hard-landscaping materials to sample due to its variability, slate slabs contain grey, rusty tones as well as red, greens, browns and black.

Basalt

If you are looking for a reliably dark clean stone, basalt is the one for you. Use it wisely in small spaces, though, as its solid dark colour will bring in spaces making them feel even smaller. Basalt is very heavy, dense and can be expensive.

Porphyry, gneiss and schist

You may find that these less-commonly used stones are not in stock when you want to purchase them so always factor in a 12–16-week lead time for your order. Variations will occur from piece to piece so be prepared to appreciate the natural beauty in the variability of these stones. That is 'designer speak' for the slabs that arrive may not look 100% like the sample you ordered from.

All stone should always be sourced from an accredited supplier who will ensure that the stone is quarried ethically.

———

'In a world where resources are becoming fewer and farther between we should be mindful about the materials we use.'

———

Drivesetts

Usually made from concrete and coloured in shades of russet, pink and grey, drivesetts are useful for hard-working areas where their tough nature helps ward off dirt from car tyres and the occasional oil spills. They are not impermeable, though; the older they get the more their surface degrades, which means that over time spillages and damage will mark surfaces permanently. Their tough nature means that they will take strong cleaning and can be jet-washed regularly to maintain their appearance. Drivesetts are very much a utilitarian surface and are best used for areas that experience high vehicle or foot traffic. If a cobbled effect is required, small-format natural stones create a more garden-like effect.

Clay pavers

Often considered to be in the same category as the concrete blocks used for driveways, clay pavers couldn't be farther away from that utilitarian concrete surface. Their hand-thrown nature results in a beautifully soft effect with subtle shade differences. Laid as a permeable surface filled with kiln-dried sand, they work in contemporary and traditional design schemes and compliment both decking and paving. From a designer's point of view, they are the perfect material for adding detail to a scheme without shouting too loudly about it. Clay pavers are understated, elegant and timeless.

Crazy paving

I may well be in the minority here but I don't think there is anything crazy about crazy paving. If we quarry stone out of our landscape, it goes without saying that we should make the most of that natural resource. If there are broken or damaged stones, why not use them as a paving material? Set fairly wide apart with their joints filled with moss or low-carpeting herbs, crazy paving stones work well with both traditional and contemporary schemes. It may seem rather outdated but in a world where resources are becoming fewer and farther between we should be mindful about the materials we use.

Porcelain

For many years porcelain was considered a poor relation to stone, a thin material that really only worked in warm climates. However, in recent years popular opinion has changed radically. There are now porcelains available that look uncannily like natural stone or wood – even if you get down on your hands and knees to take a very close look you may be fooled. Porcelain requires less maintenance than natural stone but its downside, in my opinion, is that it lacks a little bit in the 'soul' department.

Decking

Decking has had rather bad press in recent years because cheap softwood decks are liable to become slippery and degrade very quickly. However, as with any other landscaping feature, the longevity of decking materials has as much to do with their quality as it does with their installation.

Decks are ideal for roof terraces and balconies as well as ground-level town or courtyard gardens. I would be far warier of installing one in a basement space where the water table might be detrimental to its overall lifespan, though. In all cases, decks are structures built over pedestals or on a wooden framework that creates an air gap between the finished wooden surface and the ground.

Long lengths of decking are easy to transport and individually very light to carry. However, be wary of any access issues the property may have, such as tight bends or restricted headroom, as you may need to cut the decking into lengths to fit, which could result in the finished deck not looking as elegant as you wished.

Deck boards can be either smooth or reeded (grooved). Smooth-sided decking has a much nicer look but can be slippery. Reeded decking is intended to reduce slip but left unswept the grooves will collect debris that will rot down and become slippery. In essence, regular sweeping will not only make the deck look better but also prolong its life and make it far safer to walk on in wet weather.

———

'Decks are ideal for roof terraces and balconies as well as ground-level town or courtyard gardens.'

———

Soft, tactile decking is not a maintenance-free hard-landscaping option but, winding its soft wooden tones through woodland planting it is worth the effort and time required to keep it looking neat and tidy.

Softwood decking

Usually milled from pine, softwood decking is the least costly decking surface. However, it should only be used if the budget is tight because it is the most likely to degrade quickly of all the available outdoor wooden flooring surfaces. To prolong its life, apply a protective oil after installation and sweep regularly to maintain a clean, debris-free surface.

Hardwood decking

Hardwood decks are a very different beast. They should be purchased only from reputable sources that have the relevant certification to provide wood from sustainable sources. Loggers have been pilfering our rainforests for decades and there are now stringent rules in place to make sure that illegal logging does not happen. It is up to consumers to ensure that they make the correct choices when purchasing hardwood.

The timber used for hardwood decking comes in many different shades, from pale Iroko and Garapa to dark Ipe. All are variable, no two pieces of wood will be the same, even if they are from the same batch. If you would like the deck to be as uniform as possible, you may need to order a percentage extra to allow a selection process to occur.

All hardwood decks should be fixed with stainless-steel screws that are either countersunk (recessed) or via a no-screw or clipped system. Please take into consideration the fact that roof terraces and balconies often bake in direct sunlight, which means that, since wood can contract as well as expand, there will always be some movement in the timbers. As with softwood decking, there are smooth and reeded options available. Your choice will come down to aesthetics, although keep in mind that smooth decks are often easier to maintain.

If you wish to keep your rooftop decking looking rich in colour you will need to oil it regularly. Areas of decking shaded by a building or covered by furniture will change in colour less than those that are fully exposed to the sun, so you may be restricted to keeping your furniture in the same place unless you are happy to look at a patchwork-coloured floor.

Artificial decking

Yes, there really is such a thing as artificial decking – and it is worth strong consideration. Artificial deck boards are generally made from real wood that has been reconstituted into a resin and then extruded in a variety of natural – and not so natural – colours with either a reeded surface or a naturalistic wood-grain effect. If you are a purist in the wood department, this option won't be for you. However, artificial decking is a really good alternative to softwood or hardwood decking, particularly in bright sunlight where it will fade less than natural wood. In terms of maintenance, an added benefit of artificial decking is that it can be constructed over a framework made from the same material, which makes it particularly suited to basement gardens where its impermeable nature means it is less susceptible to wet conditions.

Bamboo decking

Fast-growing and very strong, bamboo is a sustainable alternative to hardwood decking. As with artificial decking, it can be encased in resin to produce strong, colour-safe boards that have little flex or movement in them. Originally only available in a dark colour, there are now many more options available. Do check the length of boards, though, as some are only offered in short lengths below 2 metres (6½ foot) long which can result in a complicated deck surface with a degree of added wastage.

Bricks and cladding

Bricks are, quite literally, the most common building block used in landscaping. Whether their presence is already felt in boundary walls or in the facade of the property, bricks in their numerous forms are commonplace. From the first gardens built millennia ago right up to the present day, bricks are part of the design legacy of our landscapes.

Whereas most paving materials can be laid capably with a medium degree of practice, building a wall is a highly skilled activity. Employing a good bricklayer will be some of the best money you ever spend in a garden – nothing will draw the eye more than a wonky joint line or, even worse, many wonky joint lines as well as bad pointing.

Reclaimed bricks

If you want your garden to have a traditional feel then reclaimed bricks will give your space an instant sense of history. However, if you think that second hand bricks will be cheaper than new bricks, think again; they often cost more, are more variable, are much harder to lay and are in restricted supply. That said, they are absolutely worth the effort and the cost.

Glazed bricks

Glazed bricks used to be the preserve of underpasses and subways but thankfully this is no longer the case. Not only will glazed bricks add colour to your garden but they also have a light-reflecting quality that can turn a dull, dark space into something very special. Glazed bricks can be formed in a conventional rectangular brick shape as well as more unusual shapes. They work well with water and artificial lighting and they lend themselves to contemporary schemes. Like reclaimed bricks, glazed bricks require specialist installation. It is worth taking time to consider the mortar colour for these because the right colour can really bring them to life.

Bricks do not have to be limited to the materials you build your house with. Blocks of all shapes and sizes can and do create textures in the garden as well as creating backdrops for lower planting.

Decorative bricks and blocks

Some people may think that the inclusion of decorative bricks and blocks in this section reveals my rather poor taste in wall materials. However, in the much the same way that I think we should be re-evaluating crazy paving, I believe that California or concrete walling, another trend from a bygone era, deserves a reappraisal. Fast to erect, this material can easily divide up a space while still maintaining a visual link between areas. A more modern approach would be to use the bricks in a staggered bond but to omit every other brick or leave vertical joints un-mortared (open perpends). The effect of this brickwork pattern on light and shadow can be breathtaking. Such walls are best left free of plants to allow them to shine in their own right.

Concrete blockwork

Even my love for concrete does not stretch to an unfinished blockwork wall. These blocks allow for the speedy creation of large walled areas that need to be clad with stone or rendered and painted. In small gardens, the large format of the blocks makes them a useful material to take through a property. The weight of concrete blockwork would be prohibitive on a roof terrace but in smaller town gardens the blocks can be used to create focal points quickly and they can even be used as a backdrop for art or water features.

The simplest way to finish a blockwork wall is with render and paint. Render is applied to a wall with a float to create a smooth surface and then exterior masonry paint can be applied in any colour of your choice – although in small spaces lighter, brighter colours will work best. Render is usually made from sand and cement but there are also textured options for added interest. Pre-pigmented renders will allow you to omit the painting stage and avoid the ongoing maintenance that paintwork requires. The colour palette for pre-pigmented renders tends to be limited but there is a good range of neutrals.

Stone cladding

Natural stone can be very useful for cladding walls as it adds warmth and a sense of luxury to a scheme. To deploy this as a finished surface, you will first need a sound and solid wall, which means that cladding existing boundary walls is generally not advisable because the weight you will be adding to the face of a wall could bring down the wall if it is 'live' (see page 94). In addition, old walls have a tendency to be wet, which means that the cladding may not adhere to the wall due to elevated moisture levels.

Stone cladding comes in easy-to-install mesh-backed units: in essence 'tiles'. The most common types of stone used for cladding are slate and quartzite in shades from cream through to black. These look incredibly attractive either as stand-alone feature elements or as strips through evergreen boundary planting. Running water over this stone surface creates movement and can be extremely effective for a water feature.

Metal

From hard and polished to soft and rusted, metal is a really useful material that can be deployed for many different applications in a garden. It not only has the ability to work as a finished surface element but can also be supremely useful when constructing features that require stability. In addition, metal panels can be used to divide up small spaces where there isn't enough room for a brick or blockwork wall.

Steel

Mild steel is a lovely material but it does rust; it may take a very long time to do so but it is not a static surface and it will degrade. Site steel features with care because the rust created from the disintegrating surface will stain anything it comes into contact with: stone, decking and even clothing if you accidentally lean against it.

Stainless steel

Stainless steel does not rust – or rather, it will not rust by itself. If stainless steel comes into contact with rust then that organic process can be transferred to its surface and is impossible to remove. Always keep mild steel and stainless steel apart to prevent transference.

Stainless steel can be mirror-polished or brushed. Both of these finishes are reflective to some degree but mirror-polished steel really does live up to its name. Consequently, it should be sited with care in a garden. It works best in dark, shady spaces where it can bounce light about. Mirror-polished steel should be used with caution on roofs and in areas of direct sunlight where the light that hits it can be refracted and concentrated – and it is not unknown for this focused light to burn nearby materials. Use it sparingly, perhaps for planters or small details within walls or to create illusions on boundary walls.

Corten steel

A rusted steel that is much-loved by designers for its warm tactile effect, Corten steel works well with softly waving banks of grasses or ephemeral perennials. Often used to clad feature walls or for laser-cut screens or pergolas, Corten steel suits both traditional and contemporary schemes. As with all metal, costs can fluctuate with exchange rates and the supply-chain timeline may sometimes be an issue, so order it in plenty of time if you intend to use it in your scheme. The warm-coloured tone of Corten steel makes it an ideal material for fire pits and burners, not least because it looks extremely attractive with flames playing over the surface at night.

Powder-coated metal

Metal can be coloured using a process called powder-coating: a powder is applied to the metal and then it is cooked to a very hard surface in an industrial oven. There are almost limitless powder finishes: smooth and textured, plain and sparkly, shiny and matt. Powder-coated metal planters, along with other metal elements in your scheme, will help to unify a small space and bring the design together. Laser-cut screening, gates and trellis will all work well in powder-coated metal. As with all pre-built elements for small spaces with limited access, do check that you will be able to carry the item through to its intended location. Failing that, consider sourcing the elements in flat-pack form and bolting the powder-coated elements together in situ.

Fences

We have touched on fences already in Design Solutions for Tricky Spaces (see page 102). There are so many things to consider when it comes to choosing fencing materials. Whether you opt for an off-the-shelf or bespoke solution, the material you select will very much depend upon whether you wish to see the fence within your scheme or would prefer it to merge into the background.

Installing a fence

Installing a panel fence or a bespoke system will take time and generate more debris than you can probably imagine. You will need a decent-size skip to remove all of the original fencing from site as well as offcuts from your new fence. Allowing ample time for setting out and installing the fence posts is essential. Once concreted in moving them will be an absolute pain, and if you have to move one then you can bet you will have to move them all. Lying the panels and post flat on the floor in front of where they will be installed if you have room will help save on tape measure-related miscalculations.

A note on fixings

If possible, always use stainless-steel fixings for fences. A nail gun may seem like a quick-and-easy answer to erecting a fence but nails will not provide the same strength and stability as screws. Nails will also mark the face of the timber as it ages.

Vertical elements can make boundaries elegant, even when they are tall and imposing.

Tanalised softwood

Tanalised wood is timber that has been treated with Tanalith, a timber preservative. The tanalisation process can leave slightly odd bright-green stains on the wood, but these will fade over time. Most softwood fences come in modular pre-sized panels that can be fitted together in different layouts, giving you some flexibility within your design. Some are simply fences, whilst others have an integrated trellis which is both decorative and practical. Although usually the least expensive form of fencing and, depending on scale, an achievable weekend project, softwood off-the-shelf fences can quickly transform a space, unify boundaries and give you a sense of achievement within your project very quickly.

Cedar

Cedar is a fast-growing softwood with a warm red tone that will fade over time. However, the timber can be oiled to retain its colour. This treatment is most effective when the fence is sited away from planting which would optimise it; once greenery takes hold the yearly task of re-oiling the fence will become difficult. Where possible, always use clear-grade cedar; it is more expensive but does not contain the knots and marks that the lower priced bracket does. Depending on how you wish your garden to look, cedar battens can be deployed horizontally or vertically in a space as they are fitted batten by batten to a bespoke post layout. This gives you flexibility, but installing a fence like this takes time and care if it is to look crisp and clean at the edges. This is a fence that will demand your full attention, both when installing and when complete.

Oak

A lovely material that lends itself to woven panels, oak fence panels can be bought off the shelf or customised to suit your site. Oak will age gracefully and eventually fade to a silvery grey. A word of advice, though: timbers can begin to turn black as part of the aging process. This black discoloration can be removed with an acid but it would be worth asking an expert to do this for you. If you are commissioning a fence from a joiner, this process should be explained to you.

Hardwood

If your fence is going to be the star of the show in your garden, hardwood fencing is well worth consideration. There are a wide variety of certified hardwoods that can be used to great effect as garden boundaries. All require a bespoke approach and a good landscaper or joiner. A hardwood fence requires stainless-steel screws or dowelled joints so that the face of the finished product is not marred by fixings. Hardwood for fences must, like hardwood for decking, only be sourced through reputable and managed sources.

Willow, bamboo and hazel

Most commonly purchased on a roll, willow, bamboo and hazel screening are all inexpensive and effective materials that can be used to cover an existing fence or wall without the expense of repairing or replacing it. Do not expect this type of screening to last for decades, it is a short term 'quick fix' that can be installed gratifyingly quickly for almost instant effect. After five years of use, especially if your fence is in an exposed area, it would be sensible to consider replacing it.

Recycled wood

Recycled wood can be used to make lovely fences with character. Such fences will never be uniform and they can be all the more attractive for it. The wood used can be myriad sizes and shapes as well as textures and colours, so although this looks like it may be a simple and inexpensive process, often the work involved in creating an effect using recycled timber can be lengthy and complicated. The effect is worth it though.

Lawn

Small gardens work hard for the space they cover and often the materials selected for them have to be thought of very much 'outside of the box'. Of all the spaces discussed in this book, small courtyard gardens are best suited to real lawn where there is access to soil beneath and drainage can be coordinated. Elevated or basement gardens do not have the luxury of natural ground underneath and consequently are either devoid of lawn or have to be greened in different ways.

Real lawn

There are many types of grass suitable for different finishes, but for town gardens, unless you really wish to be a slave to your green sward, the best grass will be tough, moderately growing varieties that require minimal ongoing care – well, minimal in terms of lawn care. If you think that a lawn needs cutting once or twice a week in the summer it actually makes it a high-maintenance element of your garden, compared to, say, trees and shrubs. Ryegrass is considered the best low-maintenance option but all grass loves sun and light to its base so scarifying to remove thatch and ensuring a good free-draining soil build-up beneath are essential elements for the success of a new lawn. Perennial weeds will always seed into turf so removing these to keep an even lawn surface is essential. Lawn is the least-expensive flooring material in a garden and some people could not consider a garden without it. That said, many small gardens are so tiny that the care required to maintain a lawn far outweighs the visual benefit of it.

Does every garden need a lawn? The short answer is not necessarily. But the swathes of reliable green that it provides sets off planting around it beautifully. It takes care to keep a lawn looking good, but the effect it creates is worth it.

'Artificial lawn has come a very long way from the astroturf of school playing fields and is now very lifelike.'

Flowering 'lawns'

The most common of these is a chamomile lawn. Ideally suited to hot dry conditions, this is really only something to try on free-draining ground in full sun and consequently is most suited to small gardens rather than basements. A lawn (or rather swathe or ground-cover planting) could also be used on a roof where the sun will benefit growth, but since there is no natural ground on roof terraces, large low planters would have to be formed and stringent calculations made to see if the roof structure could take the weight of the planting medium required. If your structure can accommodate the weight and cope with the drainage then chamomile could be replaced with one of the low-growing *Thymus serpyllum* varieties, which would be of great benefit, like the chamomile to bees and pollinating insects. Hardy enough to cope with some foot traffic it is a great way to make your roof aromatic and enticing. *Sedum spurium* varieties are also useful for green roofs and form the basis of most 'green roof' carpeting mixes. Although unscented, given very free-drainaing soil and full sun they will reward you with a rich carpet of colour throughout the year.

Artificial lawn

Yes, I do mean artificial turf. It has come a very long way from the astroturf of school playing fields and is now very lifelike with little bits of thatch woven through its plastic blades. It definitely has its place, though, and basements and roof terraces where it would be impossible to install as well as maintain real turf are viable places for this. Artificial lawns are laid on a similar base build-up to paving in most cases and can be deployed this way in basement gardens where the water table can be controlled with drainage. On roof terraces it can be laid over a waterproofed decking system that allows the roof to breathe underneath. Be warned, though, the turf can get extremely hot in full sun. No garden is ever maintenance-free and even plastic lawn needs care to keep it clean, so deploy a vacuum cleaner once a month if your lawn is small and that should keep it looking pretty tidy.

Garden lighting

What type of lighting is right for you?

You have planned your space and now you need to consider the finishing touches, of which lighting will probably be the most expensive ingredient, particularly when you take into consideration the cost of the fittings, the day rate of an electrician and the general upkeep.

The topic of garden lighting is so broad that I could write a whole book about it. Over the past ten years or so the demand for lighting in private gardens has increased exponentially. The simple reason for this increase is that we are all working longer hours and returning home later. That, combined with the larger expanses of glass that nowadays connect our inside and outside spaces, such as plate-glass windows and bi-folding doors, means that our gardens have to work very hard for us. Lighting prevents our outside spaces seeming like dark black holes when viewed from the inside of the property.

It would be very easy to provide broad-brushstroke advice about lighting gardens and say that all gardens should be lit. However, the problem is that every garden and every site is different. Some gardens in conservation areas cannot be lit. Other gardens, for example those in areas where there are no street lights, could be distracting if they were illuminated. And what type of lighting do you need? Should you use electric light or settle on candle lanterns? What is the correct answer?

If the truth be told, the answer – as with most things in the design world – is to use what works for you. Do you need lighting for security? Would you like the ambient glow of light at all times of the year or would you prefer to have the option to ramp up the drama for entertaining or special occasions?

My response when clients ask me these sort of questions is: do as much as you can to make the lighting you install flexible but also reliable – and by that I mean using the best fittings you can afford and having them installed by a qualified electrician.

If you plan to use candles then you don't need to worry about anything except avoiding putting them on or near a flammable surface. However, if you decide to use electric light outside, where rain, frost and the occasional gnawing of foxes can cause havoc, you will need to think your plans through as well as implement them carefully.

Previous page: who needs floodlights when you can create drama in a much less obvious manner? It's often the smaller details of a well lit garden that add to the overall effect and take it effortlessly from day to night. If you have limited time to enjoy your garden then extending the hours of use with good lighting is well worth it.

Right: simple, romantic, charming. You cannot go wrong with a candle and natural flame!

A comparison of light types

Electric light

- Instant effect at the flick of a switch.

- Will provide many years' use if installed correctly.

- Can be operated on a timer system to provide security.

- Many different light colours and effects are available.

- The most practical light source for modern living.

Solar light

- Requires ample sunlight to charge the lights.

- Will come on every night.

- Only has one level of light.

- Batteries are not very effective.

- Fittings tend to be clumsy.

Candlelight

- Requires some planning.

- Can only be used in fair weather.

- Burning candles cannot be left unattended as this can be extremely dangerous.

- Flames are simply flame coloured.

- Generally deemed to be the most attractive type of light and also the most atmospheric.

'It is incredible how much light it can take to highlight a plant or a tree successfully.'

Light fittings

Candle lanterns: Best used on table tops or as path-marker lights.

Uplights: Highlight trees and planting.

Downlights: Can be used on walls, steps and vertical structures such as pergolas and sheds. A subsection of downlighting is 'moonlighting', where a light is installed high in a tree to shine down and create magical shadows on the ground. For this you will need a tree without a TPO (Tree Presevation Order).

In-ground lights: Depending on their size, in-ground lights can be used to uplight large trees or illuminate steps and details in paving.

Solar lights: Best used as path markers, solar lights should be sited away from foliage and in full sun to ensure the panel receives a good charge each day.

LED strip lights: Install LED strip lights under benches or countertops. Marine-grade LED strip lights can be fully submerged in water and are ideal for lighting ponds and water features, although deploy with caution if there are fish in your pond.

Feature lights: There are now many exterior floor lamps and electric candle lanterns that can add a true indoor-outdoor feeling to a garden space. These are the kind of lights that you want to showcase in their own right. They work well around seating and dining areas.

Highlighting plants

Plants really soak up light. In fact, it is incredible how much light it can take to highlight a plant or a tree successfully. The best plants to highlight in this way are those with architectural forms. *Yucca*, *Phormium*, *Dicksonia, Phyllostachys* and *Trachycarpus* will all look dramatic when illuminated at night. Uplights (those lights that are either recessed into the ground or set on a moveable spike) are ideal for highlighting plants. Their light diffuses up the plant (often through lower-growing foliage) and softly away into the night, which means that the light does not cast great halos into the dark sky.

Urban light pollution is a huge problem for migrating birds, bats and insects so it's important to take this into consideration when designing your lighting scheme. It's also crucial to take into account the effect your lighting may have on neighbouring properties because your neighbours may not wish for their gardens to be washed with the light from your own garden.

Planning your lighting scheme

I always include a lighting scheme in any plans that I draw for my clients. The amount of light depends on the budget as well as the situation. As previously mentioned, there are some areas where you may not be able to use lights, such as conservation areas or areas of street darkness. In addition, trees with a Tree Preservation Order (TPO) cannot be lit or have lights fixed to them.

If your property is not restricted by one or more of these categories then you can begin to design your scheme.

Lighting is most effective when complimented by darkness. Not everything in your garden has to be lit at once. Think of the garden as if it were a room that needs different levels of light to create different effects. Here are some things to consider:

- Perhaps you need a base setting to highlight changes of level, steps or the bottom of walls for safety.
- Trees and architectural plants are the next setting, followed by lower-storey plants.
- Water features and sculptural items should be lit and you may wish to illuminate these elements as stand-alone pieces to create high drama.

Architectural lighting elements such as lamps are no longer the preserve of inside. Exterior options include all the fixtures and fittings interiors have to offer, making the outside a true extension of your home.

- As a general rule of thumb, I don't tend to light paving because it can be very expensive to do so. Exceptions to this rule might include a regularly used pathway to the front door or access to bins that would be tricky to negotiate without lighting to guide the way.
- Unless you absolutely love an expensive light fitting (and admittedly there are many to love), a simple casing for a light will be cheaper and the light will be the star instead.

As if all of the above isn't baffling enough, there are also different colours of light to consider. Coloured lights are an acquired taste but they can work well if used sparingly and are in tune with the overall design. They befit cutting-edge contemporary schemes and those where minimalism takes the floor. Coloured lights provide a garden with an otherworldy feel and can work to great effect when illuminating textured walling or architectural plants.

In the lighting world, there are different types of white light, just like the multiple shades of whites you will find on paint charts. However, the choice isn't onerous because there are basically two types of white light: cool and warm. In most cases, warm whites are preferred. Cool whites look great but – just like their name suggests – they have a cooling effect. Warm whites are the best choice for you if you want to feel cosy outdoors and you'd like your outdoor space to feel inviting and welcoming.

Are there particular rules for lighting small spaces?
In terms of rules, as long as you design the scheme with a light hand the result should be fine. Always err on the side of caution – you can always add more lights, but taking them away is more difficult. Adding drama where you have architectural plants or forms and contrasting those with areas with spaces where there are no lights, thereby enhances the focal point. Practical matters also take consideration with lighting and generally I would start with areas that need to be lit for safety and then add detail above that, usually on different circuits for the most amount of flexibility of use.

If you are considering using lighting in your garden and are unsure whether it is worth the outlay, first try a scheme with candles to see if the effect is something that you think will add value to the space. The next step is to contact a garden or lighting designer or a qualified electrician who can answer your questions and assist you further. Lighting is definitely not a DIY task.

Lighting tips for basement gardens
- Angle lights downwards to avoid shining light into your neighbours' windows.
- Create drama by using light to highlight architectural forms. Choose small spike lights with angled heads so you can fine-tune the effect, especially as plants grow.
- Basement spaces are dark by nature, so add light sparingly to avoid a too-bright effect.

- Avoid solar lights because they probably will not charge adequately in the shade of a basement.

Lighting tips for small town gardens and courtyards
- Light feature plants to create an enticing effect.
- Light paving only if truly necessary, if it is needed to highlight level changes or steps or as markers to a gate or to bins.
- Utilise multiple circuits to give you the greatest flexibility.
- Don't forget about candle power – it may be the answer to a soft lighting scheme in the summer.

Lighting tips for roof terraces and balconies
- Don't use uplights in paving because, with nothing above them, their effect will be lost as they shine into the sky.
- Avoid a strong light display as this will draw attention to the roof and cause conflict with neighbours.
- Try to keep light within the space to avoid unnecessary light pollution.
- Consider installing solar lights. They should charge well on a roof or balcony with good light.

Planning and implementation

'Gardens demand time and care and, no matter how well planned, there are always "unknowns" to work through, even on a blank canvas.'

The planning of your garden may take time but the actual implementing of it will take a great deal longer, even if the space is tiny. Small spaces are tricky to juggle materials around, so working out a basic schedule of what should happen when is important to keep momentum going, and also to not block you into a corner with materials that you do not need yet, and which get in the way of areas that you have to tackle first. In general terms, commencing your landscaping from the furthest point and working towards the property is the most preferred working practice. In some cases this may not be possible, in which case then stock up on heavy duty exterior floor protection to ensure that newly laid surfaces remain pristine until you have finished.

Gardens are a messy process to complete. From the initial clearance to the final wash down, every stage has elements that make what you have just completed look worse. No matter how careful you are, cleaning up at the end of each day is a necessary process, even more so in climates where overnight rain can puddle and dissolve a day's worth of landscaping dust into a gloopy grey reservoir. In some cases, if space allows, although never on roof terraces where wind is unpredictable, it may be possible to erect a gazebo to allow for dry working or alternatively in warm climates

to protect both curing materials and hot workers from the sun. Since any project outside takes time it is worth being realistic about this from the start; if you have a party or special occasion coming up and want to use the garden but time is tight – don't start. You can guarantee that the weather will immediately conspire against you and time will simply evaporate leaving you with half a completed garden that cannot be safely used. Gardens demand time and care and no matter how well planned there are always 'unknowns' to work through, even on a blank canvas. I have found more problems on new-build homes over the years than I have ever found on existing gardens. To put it simply, 'expect the unexpected' and try to allow for it time-wise if you can.

Each and every garden will be different but opposite is a guideline structure for the implementation of different types of small gardens. You will see that there are certain basics that cross over between the different types of gardens and that basements and roof terraces will take more coordination than a ground level garden. I have not accounted for any planning requirements, which you may need for roof terraces and structures in basement and town gardens. Generally speaking, it is best to allow about eight to twelve weeks for these elements.

Guideline structures for implementation, assuming that all relevant planning permissions, should you require them, are already in place:

Basement garden:

- Clear garden of all unwanted existing elements.
- Mark out the new scheme on the ground and measure for any bespoke items.
- Base up for hard landscaping.
- First-fix electrics and irrigation, if required.
- Make good all boundaries, either working with the existing or installing new.
- Install planters and raised beds if these are not to be stand-alone items over paving or other chosen hard-landscaping material.
- Crane lift or hi-ab to plant mature trees, if required.
- Install bespoke structures, water features, etc.
- Install paving or other chosen hard-landscaping surface.
- Prepare and install lawn (generally artificial).
- Final-fix electrics.
- Prepare and plant.
- Final-fix irrigation.
- Finishing touches.
- Clean down.

Small town garden:

- Clear garden of all unwanted existing elements.
- Mark out the new scheme on the ground and measure for any bespoke items.
- Base up for hard landscaping.
- First-fix electrics and irrigation, if required.
- Make good all boundaries, either working with the existing or installing new.
- Install planters and raised beds if these are not to be stand-alone items over paving or other chosen hard-landscaping material.
- Install bespoke structures, water features, etc.
- Install paving or other chosen hard-landscaping surface.
- Prepare and install lawn (generally real).
- Final-fix electrics.
- Prepare and plant.
- Final-fix irrigation.
- Finishing touches.
- Clean down.

Roof terrace:

- Clear terrace of all unwanted existing elements and bag up to be removed via a lift or stairwell.
- Ensure all balustrade to terrace edges is sound and, if not, make good.
- Mark out the new scheme on the ground and measure for any bespoke items.
- Crane lift materials up to site, if required.
- Install paving or other chosen hard-landscaping surface.
- Base up for hard landscaping.
- First-fix electrics and irrigation, if required.
- Install planters.
- Install bespoke structures, water features, etc.
- Prepare and install lawn (generally artificial).
- Final-fix electrics.
- Prepare and plant.
- Final-fix irrigation.
- Finishing touches.
- Crane lift materials down off-site or remove via a lift.
- Clean down.

Tools and materials

From a simple pen and paper to the tools of a landscaper's trade, these are a selection of the most useful items you will need to undertake your garden project.

Thinking and planning:
- Tape measure or laser measure.
- Pen and paper.
- Scale rule and ruler.
- Calculator.
- Coloured pencils.

Setting out the scheme:
- Tape measure and laser measure.
- Spirit level, preferably a 6 foot level.
- Large set square to create corners accurately (you could also work on a 3, 4, 5 triangle method).
- String line, chalk line, spray line and site pegs.
- Hammer.

Hard landscaping:
If landscaping is not your day job then you may have to hire in much of the following. Most builders merchants will be able to assist.

- Goggles, gloves, ear defenders and a first aid kit!
- Digger (if space allows) or alternatively spades, shovels, picks, wheelbarrow and sweeping-up tools.
- Cement mixer.
- Drill with wood and metal bits.
- Screwdriver.
- Grinder and stone saw.
- Wood saw (manual hand saw or chop saw, depending on how much wood you have to cut).
- Hose and jetwash.

- Paintbrushes, sandpaper, buckets and cleaner.
- Rendering float (of all the elements of hard landscaping, this is one of the few where you may wish to call in a specialist; it may look simple but rendering, like bricklaying, is a deceptively tricky and skilled process).
- Pointing tool (should you wish to tackle the brick or blockwork yourself).
- Small set square.
- Clamps.
- Packers and spacers.

Soft landscaping:
Compared to building works, planting is a gentle low-noise event and needs little in the way of machinery, unless planting large trees is on the agenda.

- Spade and fork (often border spades and forks, also known as 'lady spade or forks' are useful as they allow for smaller holes to be dug, which are useful for perennial planting).
- Hand trowel and fork.
- Rake.
- String for tying in climbing plants.

Many of the above items are only required during the build of the garden, for ongoing maintenance you may need nothing more than a yard broom, dustpan and brush (or vacuum if you have artificial turf), a pair of good secateurs, compost bag and kneepads or a kneeling mat. It is rather comforting to know that in the technological world we live in gardening can still be a simple process, not much changed from when the first hunter gatherers put down roots and began farming.

Finishing touches

Enhancing your garden space

It is the little things in life that make the big things sing. A sofa without cushions doesn't look very inviting and a table without candles or pots can look half finished. The personal elements you choose for your garden are what make it uniquely yours. These finishing touches are entirely up to you and, over time, they will most likely change with fashions and trends.

In a small space, every element needs to work hard, often serving a dual purpose.

The following clever ideas will add to your garden, not just visually but also in terms of overall utility.

Bin stores, cycle stores and sheds

Storage units can be some of the least visually appealing elements in a garden, especially in a front garden where space is often severely limited and there is no scope to create billowing areas of planting to hide the unsightly structures. Storage areas for multiple bins or bicycles, for example, take up an enormous amount of space, particularly once you've factored in the necessary free space around them to make moving the elements they contain an uncomplicated process — an especially important consideration in rainy climates, where moving large items through narrow spaces in a torrential downpour can try the patience of even the calmest person.

A great deal can be done to minimise a structure's impact on a small garden; even a simple coat of paint in a dark or neutral colour will help. Timber structures (and in the main these elements are predominantly timber) will, of course, require regular maintenance to keep them looking fresh. Another way to reduce a store's impact is to allow plants to be grown over the top to soften its appearance. This solution is of even greater importance if there is a view from above to be considered, as it is always far nicer to look down onto planting than a wide expanse of wood or metal.

If the items you are storing in the unit are valuable then it should go without saying that it is vital the structure is sound and sturdy and fitted with a heavy-duty padlock. Metal storage structures are stronger and more secure than timber ones, but they do have a slightly industrial feel, which may or may not suit your scheme.

Previous page: you probably wouldn't purchase a sofa for your lounge without trying it out first. The same goes for garden furniture; make sure it suits your space, is comfortable and the cushions are weatherproof, especially in climates where rainfall can be heavy, even in the summer.

Finding a storage solution that complements your scheme is very important. Although a mix-and-match approach can be extremely visually pleasing, in a small space less is definitely more. Any structure you select should echo the surrounding architecture and be in tune with your scheme in order to avoid it becoming a dominant feature within the garden.

In today's increasingly busy world, we shop less and less in person and home deliveries have become a normal occurrence. If you have room in your front garden, adding a storage box for deliveries while you are out can be very helpful. This could be as simple as an unlocked box or you could add a pin-code lock to it and add that number to your delivery instructions to ensure your parcel stays safe until you can retrieve it.

From a design point of view, storage helps to make a scheme practical as well as attractive, and it should always — well, almost always — be considered. There are some areas where you may fall foul of the law by adding storage elements to your front or rear gardens.

In conservation areas, for example, often it will not be possible to add anything to your garden that takes away from the historic nature of the street. It is advisable to check with the relevant authority whether there are any restrictions or if you need to apply for permission to install a large shed or bin store.

———

'Any structure you select should echo the surrounding architecture and be in tune with your scheme.'

———

Above: styling finishing touches in the same materials will ensure they blend in, especially if they are functional such as sheds and bin stores.

Log stores

Of all the possible garden storage structures, log stores tend to be the most attractive. They are generally wooden, slatted and intended for a site where they will not take the brunt of the weather. Storage structures in a rear garden tend to be hidden away but a stack of logs is visually pleasing so you could make a feature of a log store. Siting the store near the house will make running logs inside on a cold winter's day a much easier task.

Log stores can be traditional or contemporary and tend to transcend fashions and fads. Even if you don't have a log burner, fire pit or open fire, a log store can be a great home for wildlife, especially invertebrates, that can help control pests in your garden without you having to use chemical applications.

Shelves

Wall-mounted shelving and wall-hung boxes may sound like an odd thing to suggest for a garden but this kind of lightweight storage is ideal for small hand tools and plant labels. Shelves can also be used to display art or sculpture, and if situated near a barbecue or outdoor kitchen they can include racks to hold plates or cooking utensils to free up worktop space. Creating shelves will not only make your garden more usable but also allow you to personalise it to make it feel truly yours. However, before you start, it is essential that you check whether the wall in question is sound – a good landscaper can check this out for you.

Outdoor shelving needs to be made of a wood or metal that is suitable for exterior use. Whatever material you decide on, ideally it should be scratch-resistant because, no matter how tidy and pristine a garden is kept, any dirty or damaged decorative features will spoil the overall effect. Mirror-polished steel is a definite no-no for shelving unless you wish to be a slave to your duster. Slightly textured surfaces, such as wood or stone, are a better choice as they tend not to show up scratch marks or small dents and imperfections as much.

Pots and planters

Coordination of materials in small spaces is absolutely vital to the overall cohesive effect. Pots and planters are no exception. It is easy to be seduced by a lovely planter in a garden centre or nursery, in the same way that it is easy to impulse-buy a plant in flower even though you know it will not suit your site. Hardening your heart isn't easy but in the long run it will save your pocket from undue expense. By only selecting items that go together or talk to your scheme you will achieve a much better whole.

Garden designers are lovers of odd numbers and we tend to plant in threes, fives, sevens or more. Unless your scheme is very formal, where pairs of planters will work best, especially when flanking doorways and entrances, groups of odd-numbered planters will produce a softer feel. The planters can, of course, be different sizes and shapes and you can plant whatever you please in them.

Evergreens and topiary require the least amount of maintenance but it would be hard to contemplate spring without a large pot of spring-flowering bulbs somewhere. Even if the majority of your garden scheme is planted for year-round effect, if you have the time to plant your pots seasonally then you can add a lovely personal element to your garden that can reflect fashions and trends or just lift your spirits on a dull grey winter's day. If you have to carry compost and plants through the house, you may wish to opt for an evergreen only scheme so you only have to plant up the containers once. However, if you have the luxury of a side entrance then it is much easier (and a lot cleaner) to add seasonal colour to your planters.

Pests and diseases can be troublesome in small spaces where there is not much air flow or in groups of pots that can harbour slugs and snails. There are organic means of control for molluscs but if that is a bridge too far for you then try to avoid planting anything too appealing to hungry gastropods. *Hosta*, for example, are particularly susceptible to attack from slugs and snails. Instead, select plants with slightly hairy leaves or, if you have a sunny garden, choose herbs or anything else with highly scented foliage. Generally, gardening to your strengths is easier than battling an army of slugs and snails intent on munching their way through your much-loved plants.

Benches and seating

There are myriad ways to create usable and flexible seating in a garden. Some can be bought off the shelf, others need to be tailored to your space, all will add to the functionality of your garden.

Off-the-shelf seating

Shop-bought seating may be pre-built or come as a flat-pack item. Traditionally, garden furniture is made from wood but artificial rattan is now commonly available and it does not require the same ongoing maintenance as timber. Both materials have their merits so your choice will be dictated by the style of your scheme. Many furniture ranges come with complimentary storage boxes to allow the seat cushions to be kept dry when not in use. The limitation of off-the-shelf garden seating is that you may not be able to find something that is absolutely perfect for your scheme. However, with clever shopping you can create the usability that you require at a price that suits your budget.

Bespoke seating

The world is your oyster with bespoke garden furniture. Individual elements can be tailored to fit corners or difficult spaces in order to help you make the best possible use of the garden. Sofas with lift-up seating for cushion storage are really useful, especially in a rainy climate where putting cushions out and taking them in again can be more than a daily occurrence and a true chore. Customised seating can also be designed to flow with your garden style; stone and brick can be manipulated to make comfortable plinths for cushions; and wood can be used to make seamlessly elegant dual-use seating. For added appeal, it is also possible to create built-in sand pits for children's play areas that will keep the sand dry and clean. For grown-ups, wine coolers and candle holders can be fabricated within a design. The only limits to commissioning bespoke furniture are your imagination and, I am afraid, the depths of your pockets.

Right: bespoke elements do come at a price, but their integration within a design is often the catalyst for the elevation of that design above the norm, and the part they play is tenfold that of an off the shelf item if space is at a premium, which in small gardens it is.

Barbecues and fire pits

Some people are drawn like a magnet to cooking outdoors, while others are fair-weather chefs. Working out which type of person you are will dictate whether you wish to run to the expense of an outdoor kitchen or would be just as happy with a stand-alone barbecue that you can wheel out in good weather.

There are three ways to go about adding a cooking area to your garden scheme:

1. **A bespoke outdoor kitchen that is customised to your needs:** This is the option for the serious barbecue fan who wants to include grills, flavour plates, rotisseries, fridges, sinks, hot plates, teppanyaki plates, wine coolers and pretty much anything else you could wish for!

2. **An off-the-shelf barbecue:** You can buy a free-standing barbecue, including any accessories you require (such as burners, cupboards, storage, hot plates, sinks, etc.), to fit your space. This can be a less costly option. However, some barbecue ranges

'The personal elements you choose for your garden are what make it uniquely yours.'

that are available to configure can be even more costly than a bespoke built-in option. Generally, the more elegant and refined the items are the more they cost.

3. **A simple brick-built grill with a barbecue rack:** This is the kind of barbecue my family had when I was a child. This is the least attractive built-in option, but it will be the cheapest, while also being really sturdy and dependable.

Stand-alone barbecues are not beautiful items. I suspect I may antagonise some barbecue designers with that statement but I do not think they are wildly sympathetic items against a light and airy planting scheme or even against more blocky topiary and evergreens. A built-in outdoor kitchen will provide much more flexibility and can be detailed to match your scheme, including cupboards to conceal gas bottles or to hold outdoor crockery. However, this level of design and the outdoor materials required for use near consumable items do not come cheap.

If you are an occasional barbecuer then a simple gas barbecue on wheels will probably be the best choice for you. When in use, the stainless-steel nature of the barbecue will make it seem very professional. However, when covered up, which it may be for much longer than it is in use, a barbecue can be a bit of an eyesore, especially if it is sited outside the kitchen – a sensible location from an efficiency point of view. This is not a problem if you are able to wheel the barbecue out of sight when not in use but doing this often feels like a task too far at the end of the day. If you can't hide it, try siting the barbecue beside a group of pots (possibly ones containing herbs that you can use when cooking) to help it look more considered within the scheme. Just keep in mind how much heat the grill generates when it is in use. Don't put it too close to any plants, otherwise it will not only be the food you cook that becomes crispy!

———

'A water feature will generally be dictated by the style of your garden as well as your use of the space.'

———

Water features

If you type 'water feature' into an internet search engine and hit 'images' you will be confronted with hundreds of thousands of photos of different types of ponds, pools, vertical walls, bubbling puddles, sleek reflection pools and cascading urns and fountains, to name but a few. Where do you start?

A water feature will generally be dictated by the style of your garden as well as your use of the space. If your style is sleek and minimal then a bubbling puddle isn't going to work, something more along the lines of a reflection pool or vertical water wall would suit better. More natural gardens will benefit from a pond, both in terms of aesthetic appeal as well as from a wildlife-enhancing perspective.

All gardens will have restrictions on where a water feature can be placed, but basements and roof terraces even more so. Most decorative water features require a below-ground reservoir to allow water to recirculate, in basement gardens there may be no soil depth to do this in and the same goes for roof terraces where between the roof surface and the finished terrace surface there may be a very limited space (often 100mm (4 inches) or so only). It is not impossible to place water features in these locations, it is, though, more difficult to purchase off the shelf if you wish to hide the reservoir.

If the reservoir can be made a feature and stand above ground, then you will open up your search to a much broader scope. As with lights, it should go without saying that water-feature pumps are the preserve of a qualified electrician for installation. Anything where water and electrics are in close proximity should always come under the remit of a specialist.

In the same way that a hot roof terrace looks best with plants that thrive in really sunny conditions, water features tend to look most natural (even very stylised contemporary ones) with lush, leafy planting around them. Big bold leaves and water make for a very pleasing picture.

No matter where you place water in the garden it should always be safe. Recycling water features with covered reservoirs with no direct access to and depth of standing water are the safest as well as those where water simply flows in a thin sheet either down a vertical face or across an horizontal one. Natural ponds and open bodies of water are the most dangerous and can be made child-safe with a grid just under the surface. Ponds can also be made animal-safe; we think of ponds being full of amphibians but if they do not have any way to walk out of the water they will drown, so 'beach' areas or 'slipways' are vital to allow wildlife to enter and exit a pond with ease.

Other accessories

Where do you start and stop when it comes to accessorising your small garden? Ideally, less is always more, but objects that you have brought home from your travels, as well as candles and lanterns, always lend a really personal touch. Whether they are statement pieces or simply a small reminder of a happy event, much-loved items can be accommodated easily in a small garden and updating those accessories is also an easy way to ring the changes.

We've already discussed the practicalities of creating garden lighting with candles (see page 146). Candles can also serve other functions. Insect-repellent candles, for example, can be very useful in small, warm spaces, especially if your garden contains a still water feature.

If you are going to invest in a group of lanterns, it is probably worth being a bit 'designery' and creating a group of lanterns in the same style but in different sizes. For practicality's sake, keep a watertight jar of matches outside in a discreet place so you don't have to go hunting through cupboards whenever you want to light up the garden.

Votive lamps on stakes can be plunged into beds to decorate a garden. This type of lighting isn't practical on a day-to-day basis, as it is rather fiddly, but it is worth it for a special occasion when you want to create a very relaxed, romantic and intimate atmosphere.

Left: still water often sparkles with reflection and a constantly moving picture of the sky above. Consider the addition of a sculptural piece to catch the eye and minimise the open body of water.

> 'Objects that you have brought home from your travels always lend a really personal touch.'

Conclusion

I wish this book could be an all-encompassing guide to assist you with the entire process of designing gardens in small urban spaces. The truth, however, is that while the same design principles can be applied to all types of garden, no matter their shape or size, ultimately each garden will be exclusive to its owner's tastes and requirements, as well as the plot's unique site and situation. That is the beauty of gardening. Two small gardens, side by side, facing the same way, with the same environmental factors, will be markedly different because of their owners' wishes. This individuality surely makes the world a brighter and more interesting place.

A small urban garden is no more or less scary to design and implement than a large garden; it just takes thought, care and sticking to a few 'guidelines'. With this advice at the forefront of your mind, I hope you will be able to achieve everything you set out to do.

Do not be afraid to add texture to the planting in a small garden. Not all gardens have to be wildly colourful. Sometimes a muted scheme with gentle changes between the seasons can work well too.

Index

log stores 162
London plane tree 14
Lupinus 68, 69

M

maintenance 116
materials 157
 complementary 20
 contrasting 21
 coordination 163
 fencing 94, 102, 136–7
 hard-landscaping 115–41
 in keeping 57
 light-reflecting 29, 30, 35, 79
 mood boards for 19–21
 palettes 13, 14, 19–21
 and site access 45
Melianthus major 64, 65
metals 132–3, 160
mirrors 30
mood boards 19–21
mounds 96

N

nails 135
Nandina 14, 64–5
neighbours 47, 52, 82, 94, 109, 150

O

oak 137
Olea europaea 65, 88–9
oregano 88
Osmanthus fragrans 64–5

P

Paeonia 33, 68–9
paintwork 30, 130, 160
Parrotia persica 106
Parthenocissus tricuspidata 105
pathways, removal 96
paving 119–23
 laying 119
 lighting 147, 149, 150
 types 59, 120–3
 under trees 57
pedestal systems 79, 97, 119, 124
Penstemon 87, 88, 89
pergolas 76, 109
pest control 40, 42, 163
Philodendron 33, 40–1
Phormium 64, 65, 147
Phyllostachys 40–1, 64–5, 105–6, 147
Pinus 65, 88–9
Pittosporum 88–9, 106
planning 153–7

plans, scaled 12, 45, 70, 113
plants 47, 60–9
 architectural 62–4, 147, 149–50
 for basement gardens 36–41
 dealing with existing 91–9
 fast-growing 57, 79
 identification 99
 lighting 147, 149–50
 palette minimisation 29, 33, 36
 for roof gardens 79
 with softer form 66–9
pleached trees 104, 111
pollinating insects 24, 59, 140
pollution 116, 147, 150
ponds 169
porcelain 122, 123
porphyry 120, 121
powder-coated metal 132
privacy 75, 76

Q

questionnaires 12–14

R

rain shadows 52
rattan, artificial 164
reclaimed materials 59, 128, 137
render 130, 157
Rhododendron 14, 40–1
roof terraces 70–89
 design don'ts 80–3
 design dos 74–9
 drainage 97
 lighting 150
 planning and implementation 155
 plants for 84–9
 screening views 111
 structural requirements 70, 75, 76, 81
 water features 169
roofs, green 140
Rosa 33, 68, 69
Rosmarinus 88
rust 132
ryegrass 139

S

sage 88
Salvia 68–9, 88
sandstone 120, 121
sandy soil 52
Sarcococca 33, 40–1
scaled plans 12, 45, 70, 113
schist 120, 121
scope 47, 49

screening 13, 109–13
seating 164
seclusion, areas of 75, 76
Sedum 88, 89, 140
shade sails 109
shade-tolerant plants 33, 36–41, 83, 106
sheds 109, 160–1
shelves, outdoor 162
shrubs, large 106
silt 52
simplicity of design 29, 30, 57
site access 13, 45, 70, 104, 116
 through a property 13, 45, 102, 104, 116
site assessment 12–14
situation 13
Skimmia 33, 40, 41
slate 120, 121
slugs and snails 24, 42, 163
small urban gardens and courtyards 42–69
 design don'ts 56–9
 design dos 46–55
 lighting 150
 planning and implementation 155
 plants for 60–9
soft landscaping 45, 157
softwood 126, 136, 137
soil 47, 52, 82
solar lighting 146–7, 150
space, illusion of 30
speakers, exterior 30
stainless steel 132, 135
 brushed 132
 mirror-polished 30, 132, 162
starting out 10
steel 30, 132–3, 135, 162
steps/changes of level, planting under 29, 33
Stipa tenuissima 88, 89
stone cladding 130
storage 30, 160–1, 164
structural engineers 70, 75, 76, 79
structures 91–9, 109
summerhouses 109
sun-loving plants 35, 79, 106
surveys 12, 70

T

tanalised wood 136, 137
Taxus (yew) 33, 64, 65
Thymus 59, 88, 140
Tiarella 39–41, 106
time issues 13, 116
tools 157
topiary 33, 62, 64–5, 163
Trachelospermum jasminoides

109
Trachycarpus 64–5, 147
Tree Preservation Orders (TPOs) 52, 99, 147, 149
trees 106
 leaf shedding 13, 14
 lighting 147, 149
 multi-stem 64, 65
 paving under 57
 pleaching 104
 small 76
trellises 35, 94
tricky spaces 101–13
types of garden 23–89
 basement gardens 24–41, 139, 150, 155, 169
 roof terraces 70–89, 97, 111, 150, 155, 169
 small urban gardens and courtyards 42–69, 150, 155

U

use of the garden 13, 29–30

V

vertical interest 14, 59, 94, 109
views 13, 92
 masking 109–13
visual overload 19

W

wall-hung boxes 162
walls 92, 94
 boundary 52
 dominating 94
 green 14, 59, 94
 old 94, 130
 over-engineered 96
 painted 30
 rendered 30
 trellis for 35
water features 57, 130, 147, 149, 168–9, 171
waterproofing 97
wildlife 24, 42, 59, 74, 140, 147, 169
willow 137
windy sites 52, 70, 76, 81, 84, 87, 111
wish lists 47, 49
Wisteria 105

Y

Yorkstone 121
Yucca 88, 89, 147

Acknowledgements

There are so many people that I am grateful to who have influenced and enhanced the way in which I garden and who I am. First and foremost, my parents; to my Mum I owe my love of plants, growing, planting, propagating, and she is still the person that I most like to garden with. To my Dad I owe a love of making and building, the process of working out how something will be achieved even if it seems that it cannot be. I obviously owe them a lot more than this, but if we are talking gardening, then it was they who sowed the seeds of the path that I have trodden, and for that I cannot thank them enough.

Wendy Price, my tutor, encouraged me to design and garden for private clients and subtly hinted at the idea of applying to exhibit at the Chelsea Flower Show for the first time; the wisdom she has imparted upon me over the past twenty odd years has guided me more than she knows (although perhaps she does now).

Finally, this book and these words would not be here without my loyal and hardworking staff and in particular Bronwynne Britt, friend, PA, monumentally direct straight talker, arranger of flowers, maker of jewellery, lover of cocktails and life – you are one amazing lady and your contribution to how this book looks has been nothing short of awesome. You should have your name stamped all over the cover, you absolutely deserve it.

Photography acknowledgements

All photography by Helen Fickling unless marked with an asterisk

T top; B bottom; L left; R right; M: middle

Designed by Kate Gould: 2: RHS Chelsea 2017 'City Living'; 6–7 ; 18: TTL: Ascot 2018; TML ; 26–27: RHS Chelsea 2017 'City Living'; 31: All Photos RHS Chelsea 2017 'City Living'; TL: Sculpture by Michael Speller; BR: Giant Anglepoise 1227l design: George Carwardine; 37; 38: BR: RHS Chelsea 2009 'Eco Chic' ; 43: RHS Chelsea 2018 'New West End'l Furniture: Barbed.co.uk; 50–51; 53: BL; 54–55; 58: RHS Chelsea 2009 'Eco Chic'; 64: TL: RHS Chelsea 2009 'Eco Chic' ; 71; 77: BR; 85: RHS Chelsea 2017 'City Living' l Sculpture by Michael Speller; 90; 95: BL; 98: RHS Chelsea 2013 'The Wasteland'; 108: Ascot 2018; 110: BR: RHS Chelsea 2018 'New West End' l Sculpture by Michael Speller; 123: TR: RHS Chelsea 2013 'The Wasteland'; BR: Ascot 2018; 127: BL: RHS Chelsea 2017 'City Living'; 131: BL: RHS Chelsea 2017 'City Living';TR; BR: RHS Chelsea 2017 'City Living'; 133: BL; 136: BR: RHS Chelsea 2009 'Eco Chic'; 146: L; 148; 151: BL: BR; 167: L: Ceramic BBQ: Big Green Egg; 172–173: RHS Chelsea 2009 'Eco Chic'

All other gardens: 8: RHS Chelsea 2003 'Lladro Sensuality' l design: Fiona Lawrenson & Chris Moss; 11: RHS Chelsea 2018 'Spirit of Cornwall' l design: Stuart Charles Towner; 15: Watercolours by Carolyn Carter; 17: TL: RHS Chelsea 2014 'Big Green Egg' l design: Nicola Harding l build: NealeRichards for Alfresco Concepts; ML: RHS Hampton Court 2018 'Santa Rita Living la Vida 120' l design: Alan Rudden; BL: RHS Chelsea 2012 'Brewin Dolphin' l design: Cleve West; TR: RHS Chelsea 2004 'The Japanese Way' l design: Maureen Busby; MR: Field House l design: Patricia Stainton l Architects: Simon Conder Associates; BR: RHS Chelsea 2017 'Radio 2 Feel Good Gardens' l design: Sarah Raven; 18: TBL: RHS Chelsea 2009; TCTL: design: Andy Sturgeon; TCML: design: Rupert Cavendish; TCTR: design: Andy Sturgeon; TCBR: Janna Schreier Garden Design l OFYR; TTR: design: Andy Sturgeon; TBR: RHS Chelsea 2009 'Cancer Research'l design: Robert Myers; BTL: design: Chris Moss; BBL: Tony Woods l Garden Club Design; BCL: sculpture: David Harber Design; BCR: RHS Chelsea 2010 'Cancer Research' l design: Robert Myers; BTR: RHS Hampton Court 2018 'Santa Rita Living la Vida 120' l design: Alan Rudden; BBR: RHS Chelsea 2009 'Nature Ascending' l design: Angus Thompson and Jane Brockbank; 20: TL: *iStock/Nick_Pandevonium; BL: *Dreamstime.com/Ymgerman; TML: *Octopus Publishing Group/ Photographer: David Sarton/Design: Geoffrey Whiten; BML: design: Andy Sturgeon; TR: *iStock/jodiechapman; BR: *iStock/Barcin; TMR: design: Hadrian Whittle l Filmscapes; TBR: design: Amir Schlezinger l Mylandscapes; 21: TL: design: Matt Keightley; BL: design: Tony Woods l Garden Club Design; TML: *Dreamstime.com/Meepoohya; BML: design: Chris Moss Gardens; TR: Chelsea 2015; BR: design: Tom Hoblyn; TMR: design: Tom Stuart-Smith; BMR: design: Tom Prince & Alex Frazier - LDC Design; 22: RHS Chelsea 2014 'Big Green Egg' l design: Nicola Harding l build: NealeRichards for Alfresco Concepts Ltd; 25: Nina Reinhardt Landscapel architect: Paul Archer Design; 32: TL: BL: BR: Nina Reinhardt Landscapel architect: Paul Archer Design l furniture: Barbed.co.uk; TR: RHS Chelsea 2006 'Cancer Research'l design: Andy Sturgeon; 38: ML: *iStock/igaguri_1; TL: *iStock/49pauly; TC: *iStock/seven75; MC: design: Andy Sturgeon; 41: TL: *GAP Photos/Jonathan Buckley; ML: The Palm Centre; BL: The Palm Centre; BM: *iStock/AlpamayoPhoto; MR: *Alamy Stock Photo/Rob Whitworth; 44: RHS Hampton Court 2018 'B&Q Bursting Busy Lizzie Garden' l design: Mathew Childs; 48: RHS Chelsea 2018 'Urban Flow' l design: Tony Woods l Garden Club Design; 53: TL: RHS Chelsea 2014 'Big Green Egg' l design: Nicola Harding l build: NealeRichards for Alfresco Concepts; TR: RHS Chelsea 2015 'Homebase Urban Retreat' l design: Adam Frost; BR: design: Chris Moss; 61: design: Catherine Heatherington; 63 RHS Chelsea 2011 'The Australian Garden RBGM' l design: Jim Fogarty; 64: BL: design: Raymond Jungles; TM: design: Matt Keightley; TMC: design: Kevin Young l Garden Wise; BMC: design: Tom Stuart-Smith; TR: design: Andy Sturgeon; TMR: BMR: BR: RHS Wisley; 67: design: Chris Moss Gardens; 68: TM: design: Clare Agnew; TMC: design: Philip Nixon; BMC: design: Chris Beardshaw; BM: design: Chris Moss Gardens; 72–73: design: Andy Sturgeon; 77: TL: design: Miria Harris; BL: Field House l design: Patricia Stainton l architects: Simon Conder Associates; TR: design: Haruko Seki - Studio Lasso l architects: Michaelis Boyd Associates; 78–79: design: Andy Sturgeon; 86 ML: *iStock/imv; BL: design: Andrea Fawcett Phillippart; TM: design: Alan Rudden; CM: design: Terence Conran & Nicola Lesbriel; TR: *iStock/CharlesGibson; MR: design: Tom Prince & Alex Frazier; 89: TL: design: Chris Moss Gardens; BM: design: Andy Sturgeon; 38: MR: The Palm Centre; MR: design: Diarmuid Gavin & Terence Conran; 93: RHS Chelsea 2009 'Daily Telegraph' l design: Ulf Nordfjell; 95: TL: RHS Chelsea 2014 'Mind's Eye Garden RNIB' l design: Tom Prince & Alex Frazier; TR: RHS Chelsea 2017 l design: Teo Architects - TetraH Wall; BR: design: Janna Schreier l OFYR; 100: design: Philip Nixon; 103: RHS Chelsea 2018 'Spirit of Cornwall' l design: Stuart Charles Towner; 104: L: RHS Chelsea 2012 'Laurent Perrier Bicentenary' l design: Arne Maynard l sculpture by Breon O'Casey, entitled: 'Stylised Bird'; R: RHS Chelsea 2009 'Telegraph Garden' l design: Ulf Nordfjell; 105: Field House l design: Patricia Stainton l architects: Simon Conder Associates; 106: RHS Chelsea 2007 'Westland'l design: Diarmuid Gavin & Stephen Reilly l Rooms Outdoor; 107: design: Amir Schlezinger l Mylandscapes; 110: TL: RHS Hampton Court 2018 'Santa Rita Living la Vida 120' l design: Alan Rudden; BL: RHS Chelsea 2004 'Hortus Conclusus' l design: Christopher Bradley-Hole; TR: RHS Hampton Court 2018 'RNIB' l design: Steve Dimmock & Paula Holland; 112–113: RHS Chelsea 2011 'Cancer Research UK' l design: Robert Myers; 114: RHS Hampton Court 2018 'Santa Rita Living la Vida 120' l design: Alan Rudden; 117: TL: RHS Chelsea 2006 l design: Dean Herald l Flemming's Nurseries; BL: RHS Chelsea 2009 'Marshalls Living Street' l design: Ian Dexter; TR: RHS Chelsea 2017 'M&G'l design: James Basson; BR: RHS Chelsea 2018 'Urban Flow' l design: Tony Woods l Garden Club Design; 118: design: The Garden Makers l Furniture: Barbed.co.uk; 120: TL: BR: design: Tom Stuart-Smith; ML: design: Andy Sturgeon; BL: design: Tom Price & Alex Frazier; TR: design: Hadrian Whittle l Filmscapes; MR: design: Jack Merlo l Flemming's Nurseries; 123: TL: *iStock/Nico_Campo; BL: design: Tony Woods l Garden Club Design; 125: RHS Chelsea 2009 'Nature Ascending' l design: Angus Thompson & Jane Brockbank; 127: TL: design: Chris Beardshaw; TR: *Elite Baulstrade, www.elitebaulstrade.com; BR: design: Tom Prince and Alex Frazier; 129: RHS Chelsea 2010 'Daily Telegraph' l design: Andy Sturgeon; 131: TL: design: Alan Rudden; 133: TL: Festival International des Jardins l Chaumont sur Loire l design: Daniel Jud & Phillippe Herlin; TR: design: Andy Sturgeon; BR: design: Kathryn Hibberd l 12 Garden Design; 134: RHS Chelsea 2010 'Cancer Research' l design: Robert Myers; 136: TL: RHS Chelsea 2009; ML: design: Andy Sturgeon; BL: design: Christopher Bradley-Hole; TR: design: Chris Moss Gardens; MR: design: Kevin Young l Garden Wise; 138: RHS Chelsea 2014 l design: Tommaso del Buono & Paul Gazerwitz; 141: BL: RHS Chelsea 2009 'Daily Telegraph'l design: Ulf Nordfjell; TR: RHS Chelsea 2012 'Rainbows Children's Hospice' l design: Chris Gutteridge, Ant Cox & Jon Owens; BR: RHS Chelsea 2005 'In the Grove' l design: Christopher Bradley-Hole; 142: RHS Chelsea 2012 'Arthritis Research UK' l design: Thomas Hoblyn; 145: design: Louise Cummins l The Garden Makers; 146: TR: RHS Chelsea 2009 'Laurent-Perrier' l design: Luciano Giubbilei; BR: design: Wynniatt-Husey Clarke; 151: TL: design: Andy Sturgeon; TR: Hampton Court 2008 'The Spirit's Garden' l design: Jill MW Foxley; 152: *iStock/andreaskrappweis; 156: *iStock/cjp; 158: RHS Chelsea 2018 'Morgan Stanley - NSPCC' l design: Chris Beardshaw; 161: RHS Chelsea 2009 'Children's Society' l design: Mark Gregory; 162: L: RHS Chelsea 2009 '1984' l design: Chris Gutteridge, Antony Cox & Jon Owens; R: design: Ecospace.com; 163: L: design: Andy Sturgeon; R: RHS Chelsea 2015 'Telegraph Garden' l design: Marcus Barnett Studio; 164: L: design: Andy Sturgeon; R: RHS Chelsea 2012 'M&G' l design: Andy Sturgeon; 165: RHS Chelsea 2012 'Trailfinders'l design: Jason Hodges l Flemming's Nurseries; 166: L: RHS Chelsea 2016 'Telegraph Garden' l design: Andy Sturgeon; R: RHS Chelsea 2018 'Urban Flow' l design: Tony Woods l Garden Club Design; 167: R: RHS Chelsea 2010 'Kebony' l design: Darren Staines; 168: TL: RHS Chelsea 2012 'Laurent-Perrier Bicentenary' l design: Arne Maynard; BL: design: Catherine Heatherington; TR: RHS Chelsea 2008 'Laurent-Perrier'l design: Tom Stuart-Smith; BR: RHS Hampton Court 2018 'Santa Rita Living la Vida 120' l design: Alan Rudden; 170: design: Thomas Hoblyn l Artist: Rick Kirby 'The Call'; 171: L: design: Chris Moss Gardens; R: Creator of concrete hand, unknown.